JACKIE CHAN

Edited by
John R. Little and Curtis Wong

CB

CONTEMPORARY BOOKS

Library of Congress Cataloging-in-Publication Data

Little, John R., 1960–.
    Jackie Chan / John R. Little and Curtis Wong.
        p.   cm.
    Filmography: p.
    ISBN 0-8092-2837-8
    1. Motion picture actors and actresses—China—
Hong Kong—Interviews.   I. Wong, Curtis.
II. Title.
    PN2878.L465 A3   1998
    791.43′028′092—dc21
    [b]   98-17958
                                      CIP

Cover design by Todd Petersen
Cover and interior photographs courtesy of CFW Enterprises
Interior design by Amy Yu Ng

Published by Contemporary Books
A division of NTC/Contemporary Publishing Group, Inc.
4255 West Touhy Avenue, Lincolnwood (Chicago), Illinois 60646-1975 U.S.A.
Printed in the United States of America
International Standard Book Number: 0-8092-2837-8

99 00 01 02 03 04 VL 19 18 17 16 15 14 13 12 11 10 9 8 7 6 5 4 3 2 1

This book is dedicated to all martial artists and future filmmakers who are open-minded enough to learn from others, and passionate enough to create something new. And especially to two of Jackie Chan's biggest "little" fans, Riley and Taylor, and one big fan, Muskoka's own "Millionaire" Marty Rhodes.

Contents

Foreword

Words, opinions, ideas, and statements always have more meaning when they come directly from the source, rather than when they've been run through the filter of a second or third party's personal opinion or conditioning. To this end, *Inside Kung-Fu* has enjoyed the very privileged position among martial arts publications of being able to bring to its readers Jackie Chan's own words, opinions, ideas, and statements about his life, art, and career.

Whereas other magazines have had to rely on "insider" opinions, prejudices, and preferences in bringing their readers more information on Jackie, we've been able to go to the source—Jackie Chan—directly, and frequently, over the past twenty years. To this end, we have amassed a considerable database of direct quotes, insights, and personal beliefs from Jackie that, when taken together, form a complete picture of the true Jackie Chan. For those who may never have had the opportunity to sit down and speak one-on-one with Jackie, this book is our attempt to share with you just what this unique experience is like. You will see as you pore over the pages of this book that Jackie Chan is a very eloquent man. He speaks seven languages and communicates thoroughly, engagingly, and succinctly. He is also very intellectually and emotionally stimulating, as he will speak his mind, even if that means cutting firmly against the grain of popular opinion or political correctness. This makes him that most rare of human animals—the honest man.

To this end, we at *Inside Kung-Fu* would be doing a grave disservice to this remarkable man if we simply attempted to cobble together a series of articles that featured third-party descriptions of Jackie Chan or simply reviews of his films. Although some other recent books have done just this, we believe that this ultimately avails the reader nothing that is enduring or redeeming about the man himself. To this end, our intention with this book has been to comb through all of the interviews that Jackie Chan has graciously granted to the publications under the banner of CFW Enterprises (chiefly *Inside Kung-Fu* and *Martial Arts Legends*) over the years, and select from them the statements that we felt best reflected the soul of the man and his beliefs on a wide range of topics that most of his fans—as well as those new to Jackie Chan—are most interested in. Where necessary we have probed deeply, asking him questions about God, success, peace, and his self-imposed role as an ambassador of global goodwill, his considerable work for charity, and his views on racial tolerance and social responsibility.

Being a martial arts publication, we have also recognized Jackie's immense talent and experience in this realm. We have asked him to share his views on the state of martial arts today, his own training in the arts, and what techniques he has found to be the most useful and practical over the years. We believe that his answers to these questions will prove very useful to all martial artists. And then there is the issue of health and fitness—how is a human being capable of performing all of the incredible stunts and martial arts/action sequences that Jackie Chan has demonstrated to us year after year? What does he do to keep in shape both at home and on the road to create and maintain such an incredible peak of condition?

This book will reveal to you—in Jackie Chan's own words—why he is who he is and how he came to be that way. His words will inspire and educate you, and, more important, you will come to know Jackie Chan—the real Jackie Chan—in a deeply personal way, rather than in the often cold and detached manner that many film critics and magazine scribes use.

John Little (left) visits with Jackie on the set of *Rush Hour*.

We believe that when you are finished with this book, you will have come to appreciate and respect Jackie Chan in a way that transcends his considerable physical prowess. You will come to appreciate his mind, his dedication to excellence in filmmaking, and above all his love for people of all races and religions. In other words, you will come to know, respect, and love Jackie Chan—the man behind the legend—as we at *Inside Kung-Fu* have for well over two decades.

—John R. Little

Preface

I'm proud to say that I count Jackie Chan among my closest friends. For well over two decades I've attended premieres of his films with him, taken cruises with him and his family, and even traveled to the sets of his films to watch him perform his unique blend of action and comedy firsthand.

But the times spent with Jackie that I really treasure are the less public times that we've spent alone talking about life, movies, his concerns regarding children, and the martial arts. Through all of these experiences I've come to know the real Jackie Chan—the human being behind the legendary international action star— and it is this Jackie Chan I would like you to experience through the pages of this book.

My company, CFW Enterprises, has published many martial arts magazines over the years, including *Inside Kung-Fu* and *Martial Arts Legends*. Jackie has always been good to these publications. In fact, when he first granted us an interview, we were a fledgling publication. Then, like now, Jackie could have spoken to any publication he chose. For reasons that only he will ever know, he chose mine. Whenever he came to town, Jackie would always be gracious enough to sit down and talk about his life and what incredible things were happening in it. And fortunately for us, and for posterity, I always made sure that I had our reporters present to record it. For then, like now, it was obvious to me that there was indeed something special about Jackie Chan.

You have to understand that through the course of a typical year, Jackie Chan speaks to hundreds, perhaps even thousands, of journalists from all over the world about his latest films—what it's like working with certain actors, filming in exotic locales, and the high risk of his incredible stunts. But, unlike *Inside Kung-Fu* and *Martial Arts Legends*, these journalists will then typically move on to their next superstar, their next assignment, and promptly forget about the incredible man they have just had the opportunity to speak with. I've read many of their articles, too, and they've never once done more than simply scratch the surface of what Jackie Chan is all about. I feel fortunate in that the writers employed by my publications have been able to spend so much more time with Jackie than these other writers and have always sought to ask the deeper, more substantial questions. His phenomenal physical prowess stopped being the motivation for our coverage of his career a long time ago—we always were more interested in the man behind the persona. Besides, as far as stunts go, we covered most of these—as they happened—over a span of some twenty years. The fact that he is the preeminent action star and top-level martial artist is old news to us. More important, Jackie is our friend, and his ideas and opinions are always fascinating to us, whether they be on his life experiences, his philosophy, his views on racism or religion, how he keeps in shape, his incredible body of work, or his hopes for the future. With all the major media attention paid to some of our American action heroes these days, it strikes me that many of them are copies, not originals. And the man they are copying the most these days is Jackie

Left to right: Solon So, Willie Chan, Jackie Chan, Curtis Wong, and Kenneth Lo during a break in shooting for *The Jackie Chan Story* documentary at Santa Monica Pier.

Chan. Jackie is the genuine article, a man who cares deeply about his craft and an artist of the highest order.

That is why when Contemporary Books approached John Little and me about collecting the best articles and photos and releasing a special five-book series to commemorate the milestone of our twenty-fifth anniversary in the martial arts publishing business, the first name that came to my mind was Jackie Chan. Here was our chance to say "thank you" to a man who has always given so freely of his time to us and to pay a respectful, long-overdue tribute. This also was our chance to introduce the real Jackie Chan to America for the first time. John and I could have kicked off this series with any action hero over the past twenty-five years—for we have featured articles on all of them, from Chuck Norris and David Carradine to Steven Seagal and Jean-Claude Van Damme. But I wanted the first book in this series to be something special and unique, and stand head and shoulders above the rest—something like Jackie Chan himself.

I hope you have as much fun getting to know the real Jackie Chan through the pages of this book as I have had knowing him personally over the past twenty years.

—Curtis F. Wong

Chairman, CFW Enterprises

Publisher, *Inside Kung-Fu* magazine

Acknowledgments

We would like to thank Jackie Chan for his time and genius, Willie Chan for his patience, and Golden Harvest and Media Asia for all of the assistance they have provided throughout the years.

Introduction

Jackie Chan was born in Hong Kong on April 7, 1954, and named Chan Kong Sang. He was brought into the world by a family so poor that he was almost sold at birth to the British doctor on duty for twenty-six dollars!

The Chans kept their only child with them until after their emigration to Australia, where Chan's father worked full-time as a chef, his mother as a maid. Boarding the feisty youngster back in Hong Kong was a practical choice. An opera school seemed like a good match.

Chinese Opera School

The youngsters in a Chinese opera school were groomed to take part in a centuries-old "folk art" theatrical tradition of various playlets and performance pieces, some more popular in one region than another, many of them with military themes. For the latter, fighters in painted faces and colorful costumes, accompanied by drum and gong and cymbals, had to whirligig across the stage in stylized acrobatic ballets.

This mixture of fighting and dance is less strange than it may appear to Western eyes. According to legend, at least one famous Shaolin rebel of the 1600s took refuge from the Manchus by joining an opera troupe, among whose onstage combats it was possible to conceal and preserve true "secret fists" styles. In Chinese communities, opera held a broad-based audience appeal until the late 1960s. The Chans were advised on a school for their boy in 1961.

So Jackie Chan began to learn kung fu in Hong Kong at the age of seven and a half. The child anticipated nothing but fun when he signed himself up for the longest possible course at the China Drama Academy (Opera Research School), an institution geared to turning out the elite in martial arts performers. But there, under master Yu Chan Yuan, the students lived in an atmosphere akin, in Western terms, to that of a grim Charles Dickens novel. Traditional kung-fu training was taken so seriously that beatings were common. Days were nineteen hours long, and the curriculum was comparably exhaustive.

Under several different masters, Chan studied virtually every Northern Shaolin system [of kung fu] that has survived into the modern era. These systems consist of myriad techniques. And since they include an emphasis on long-range strategies expressed through fluid groundfighting movements, Chan also studied gymnastics and acrobatics. A painful leg-training session was an everyday experience, as was weapons practice, even for the very young.

Although reading and writing received scant attention, each student learned miming and the basics of acting. They learned to sing by screaming at a brick wall. By means just this side of torture, they acquired the additional circus and magiclike skills demanded by Chinese opera and by Master Yu.

A Child Actor at Age Ten

Through all of these activities, Chan became so accomplished that by the age of ten he was doing child parts in dramatic films. He attracted much attention as well from the audiences at the live "Peking Opera" shows presented by the school. Stage-named Yuan Lou, Chan traveled throughout Southeast Asia for the school as one of the "Seven Little Fortunes" ("Seven Little Favorites"), a troupe that included stars and moviemakers-to-be Sammo Hung and Yuen Biao, directors-in-the-making Corey Yuen (Yuen Kwei) and Mang Hoi, and two other boys likewise destined for the big time as film performers and martial arts directors in Hong Kong.

Because Master Yu was entitled to keep as tuition by far the greater portion of the earnings from these early movie jobs and shows, he paid Chan and his "kung-fu brothers" only meager amounts of spending money. Chan stayed with the program for seven more years, ten years of fighter-cum-entertainer training in all. As the period drew to a close, he began working as a stuntman and assistant martial arts choreographer known as Chen Yuan Long (Main Dragon Chan), while his "elder brother" Sammo Hung was known as Yuan Long (Main Dragon).

All together now: Three close friends and Hong Kong movie giants. From left: Sammo Hung, Yuen Biao, and Jackie Chan, who teamed to make some of the top Golden Harvest movies of all time. This rare scene was taken from *Project A.*

Meanwhile, Chan was experimenting with hapkido and tae kwon do; he was picking up tricks from Southern Shaolin styles of kung fu and from his own fertile improvisatory brain.

How to "Die" Dramatically

By age eighteen, when Chan was instructing other martial artists in performing for the camera, he was particularly capable of teaching how to fall and how to "die" dramatically. According to popular lore, Chan's acting was "discovered" while he was coaching a key actor's death scene, demonstrating how a bitter end ought to look. A stray producer preferred Chan's manner; so Chan played his first hero in 1971. But the film, *Little Tiger from Canton*, made a mere growl at the box office.

At the same time, Chan's nose had, literally, preceded the rest of his body into maturity. Still in his teens, he hadn't yet attained his full 5′10½″, 153-pound frame; yet it was clear enough why other kids always called him "Big Nose."

In the next few years, Chan's shifting moods and fortunes passed him back and forth between happening Hong Kong and sleepy Canberra, Australia, where his parents had settled. Then in 1976 a young "filmplanner" named Willie C. K. Chan (no relation), the same Willie Chan who remains Jackie's manager to this day, brought the young talent to the attention of producer Lo Wei. As the director of the first two films of the late worldwide phenomenon Bruce Lee, Lo had set up a new production company. He promptly "adopted" Jackie Chan as his godson and signed him to a multipicture deal.

Chan Was Not the "Next Bruce Lee"; He Was the First Jackie Chan

Undoubtedly remembering Lee as "Little Dragon," Lo changed Chan's professional name to Cheng Long, or Sing Lung in Cantonese (which roughly means "potential dragon," or "one becoming a dragon"). Thus began a ten-film arrangement, at the start of which, using Chan's prodigious gifts, Lo attempted first to clone the inimitable Lee and then to pour Chan's mercurial skills into an imitation Shaw Brothers "martial chivalry" mold. Although these efforts caused a movie-business buzz about Lo's now English-named "Jackie" Chan, there were no great commercial rewards.

In 1978 a perplexed Lo Wei loaned Chan out to Seasonal Films, where producer Ng See Yuen, director Yuen Woo Ping, and Jackie Chan collaborated on two films. In the first, Chan starred as a humble boy-man, in the second as an arrogant scamp. In both films his wily and chastening costar was the director's father, Simon Yuen (Yuen Hsiao Tien). For additional chemistry, the elder Yuen had also been a real-life master of Chan—the only even-tempered one, it's said—at the China Drama Academy in Hong Kong. *Snake in the Eagle's Shadow* and *Drunken Monkey in a Tiger's Eye* (more popularly known as *Drunken Master*) hit the local box office with a heavyweight one-two punch, firmly establishing a new subgenre—"comedy kung fu." Few other creative teams had ever tried kung fu and comedy. Chan's almost-leading-man looks and unmatched physical abilities were what it took to make the new breakthrough combination.

The Rise of Kung-Fu Comedy

Although true stardom had seemed slow to come, Chan was well equipped to obtain and then maintain it. He'd had a love-hate relationship with the course of

Jackie combined liberal doses of action and comedy in the film *Project A.*

In *Spiritual Kung Fu,* Jackie blended time-honored forms with vignette parodies of martial arts moves.

study at the opera school, but the headmaster's discipline (as Chan would later respectfully and grudgingly admit) paid off in eight of the martial arts movies he completed from 1976 through 1981: *Shaolin Wooden Man*, *Snake and Crane Arts of Shaolin*, and *Spiritual Kung-Fu*, the two comedy kung fu films from Seasonal Films, and the three directed by Chan himself: *The Fearless Hyena*, *Young Master*, and *Dragon Lord*.

Chan performed handsome, neoclassical combinations of martial arts moves (kata) for the first two on this list and for Seasonal Films. For all the latter five films, he put forth a superabundance of techniques and humor, an array of traditional fighting styles replete with multiple kicks, strikes, and punches at triple tempo. But he was not content to be the Baryshnikov of battery. Chan showed complete mastery over a veritable zoo of animal styles, and when these wouldn't take him where he had to go in a fully developed fight scene, one of his ingenious exaggerations or improvisations would.

Chan blended time-honored forms with training esoterica and vignette parodies of martial arts moves that sent him tumbling, sprawling, and churning across the screen. He briefly set up a definite rhythm of strikes and rebounds, then pushed that pattern way off the beat. His baroque and even dizzying displays of athleticism flowed swiftly and hilariously before the wide-open eyes of his growing, spreading audience.

They had to laugh, and they had to love him. Within a thirty-minute segment of *The Fearless Hyena*, for instance, Chan flipped through some Hung Gar, an assortment of open-hand techniques, some Wing Chun, classical stances such as fist-on-hip, White Crane leg movements, inventions such as the transposition of Wing Chun arm movement concepts to his legs, a chopsticks battle, and the esoteric upside-down sit-ups training exercise. Ceaselessly, he used everything he had, psyching opponents with his putty face, rubber legs, and steel muscles.

By the beginning of the 1980s, the mix defied comprehensive description. Chan had to summarize it simply as "my own style." And not even he could say where his nonstop novelties were coming from. But any Far East moviegoer could tell where all of this was headed: Jackie Chan could take a long lease on that room at the top of the box-office charts. As the 1980s began, American fans caught Chan using the old to make the new. Close observers saw him tip that funny gray hat in *The Fearless Hyena* and *Young Master* to 1920s comic Ben Turpin. Most of those who wrote about the arriving "King of Kung Fu" compared his fleet-footed derring-do to Hollywood stars of bygone days, to Errol Flynn, to Douglas Fairbanks, or to the three "little guy" giants of the silent era: Charlie Chaplin, Buster Keaton, and Harold Lloyd.

Chan's offscreen image supported the linkage to the great physical comedians. American marketers of the 1980 Warner Brothers release *The Big Brawl* showed some confusion about what to sell and how to sell it. But to reporters in the United States, Chan spoke freely about his desire to stay away from the heavy-breathing ferociousness, vengeance, and bloodshed that swamped Hong Kong martial arts movies in the wake of Bruce Lee's triumphs. Bruce Lee imitators don't make it, he shrewdly observed. He wanted to act in and direct action movies with human emotion and drama that families would enjoy. "I'm not a big, violent person," he told Tony Page, a Hong Kong–based reporter for a U.S. magazine. "I like playing

The success of all of Jackie's films ultimately rests upon his shoulders alone. Here he supports a weight of a different sort in *Young Master*.

underdogs, little humble people. I'd like to be seen as a Dustin Hoffman who can fight. If I win, I'm lucky."

To offset the hard-edged, karate-ized fight stylings that were the best Hong Kong's post–Bruce Lee pretenders could come up with, Chan had already added the "fancy" traditional kung fu he described as requiring painstaking precision and timing to get across on film. And he had added comedy. Provided there was a serious midpoint fight and a serious final fight, the new formula he was cooking ought to work, he figured—especially with a comic tag at the end to send the audience out of the theater upbeat and buzzing.

Validation came with the unprecedented commercial success of *Young Master*, which ended with a visual quote from an earlier Chan hit, revised to leave Chan himself in casts and bandages from head to toe. As a filmgoing experience, this last little scene was indelible: the "winner" Jackie Chan, his two blackened eyes sparkling out through a peephole in his mummylike wrappings, waving bye-bye to the viewer while his sound track voice sang "Kung Fu Fighting Man" and the credits rolled. Here was a hero worthy not of the title and the championship belt, but of two months of traction at the local hospital. The final frames of *Young Master* were odd. They were a hoot. They were also a foreshadowing.

Success Begets Power

His first big hit, in 1978, had made Chan living proof that, in addition to payment in money, success gets paid in power. Power had set the new star free to design and direct his own projects, to make changes, to become a target on the move ahead of his closest Hong Kong competitors, then to succeed again, and to repeat the process in a cycle that Chan continues today. To whatever degree this circular chase may be self-fulfilling, it also accurately reflects the round of creativity and commerce that moviemaking is, wherever it occurs.

At work in 1981 on *Dragon Lord* (1982), Chan was constantly mixing motifs from East and West as well as old and new. Silent comedy–style, Chan's hero "Dragon" met challenges more than a few feet off the ground. Sports, as *Martial Arts Movies* writer Kenneth Haker noted, figured largely in the film: teams of youths hand-charged a prize atop a pagoda of buns and played a Western-flavored cross between shuttlecock and soccer.

For any fights, Chan told movie magazines at home, he instructed his stuntmen that they could hit anywhere, anytime. Why? "Because this movie has to be the best." And what did "the best" entail? Convinced he knew the secret of his own success, Chan dedicated himself then and ever after to two principles—innovation and authenticity. If Jackie Chan were a Shaolin graduate getting those famous tattoos in this age, one of his forearms would say "Innovation" where in days of yore a dragon would be, and the other would say "Authenticity" instead of showing a tiger.

Jackie's Art of Reality Filmmaking

Although *Dragon Lord* was set in the familiar Ching Dynasty period, then thought to be favored by Chan's Asian audiences, its filmmaker-star set forth on the road to realism. Hong Kong moviemakers had learned noncontact fight choreography from the visiting American production of *The Sand Pebbles* in the early 1960s. But Chan now returned to the visceral energy, not to mention publicity value, of trading real blows. From the production point of view, there's some logic in the plan. Chan could use multiple cameras to shoot simultaneously from several angles without revealing the "misses" between the kicks and punches—because there were no misses!

Some sections of fight scenes were put on film faster and easier this way. But Chan still took months, shot 360,000 feet of film (around three times the norm), and had ninety stuntmen hitting the Taiwan dust, then hitting the emergency room. In key scenes, Chan had stopped using mats to break falls, whether his own or his stuntmen's. Trampolines were out, as were most other live special effects. Hong Kong filmers had never had much infrastructure of live special-effects technicians anyway, or of mechanical riggings other than the belt-and-wire devices used for "wire work" in "flying people" for swordplay movies. "Realism" was the most affordable way to go, and it was readily accessible in Chan's hand-picked team of expert stuntmen. Then, as before and even now, Chan did his own fights and stunts, making sure to get at least one good take to authenticate his face atop his freewheeling body in every bit of risky business. When *Dragon Lord* did well at the box office, Chan's shift to realism seemed to have audience support.

Set in the city of Hong Kong in the late 1800s, Chan's *Project A* (1983) has the Coast Guard against the pirates for a less provincial feel than ever before. Chan crowded some Western boxing back into his melees and crowded a lot of

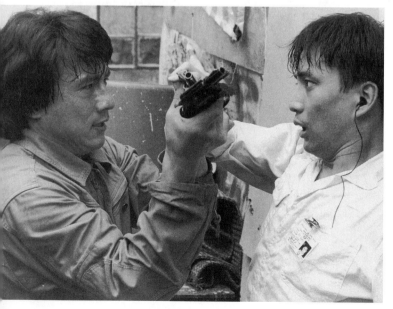

Jackie adds the real-world element of guns to his films, not relying simply on hand-to-hand combat.

traditional kung fu back out. As in *Dragon Lord*, his focus was often on multiman fights. He explained to *Inside Kung-Fu* that "more is better."

The use of several opponents compels a fast tempo and packs the action. He told another American publication that these "modern" fight sequences showed his progress in developing a distinctive filmfighting style, in addition to being easier to do. Much later, Chan went back over the *Dragon Lord/Project A* juncture in his career for *L.A.Weekly* film journalist David Chute, speaking first about his escape from the rigor mortis of established kung-fu movie genres. Then, he said, "About that time I saw a lot of Buster Keaton films. He gave me a lot of ideas, new things I could do that were physical, and funny, but were not fighting."

Inserting Outtakes into His Films

By the time *Project A* was finished, it was obvious that Chan had immersed himself in the silent comedy masters. Most notable was his clock-tower homage to Lloyd's *Safety Last* (1923). That scene provided Jackie's first world-class accident, his more than fifty-foot plunge through a first awning and horrifying flip off the frame of a second awning to land on his head, not on a mat, of course, but right on the street below. The occasion was instantly famous. And it was instantly replayed; takes from multiple cameras cut one after another directly into the body of the film, for some moments derailing conventional narrative flow, as Hong Kong cinema critic Tony Rayns pointed out. And with the multiple-cut showcase, the Jackie Chan movie became a "Jackie Chan documentary," film reviewer Dave Kehr agreed.

This documentary aspect was lightheartedly expanded for the final credits, as Chan had seen done in *The Cannonball Run* (1981). The end of *Dragon Lord* had the biggest movie star in Asian history flubbing stunts. Here was evidence that, his Superman ease and grace apparently under some Kryptonite curse, Jackie Chan had blown bit after bit and then yowled in pain or cracked up laughing, just like the regular guy his audiences knew he was. Just like a superstar. Of all the outtakes, the one that got the loudest gasps was the clock-tower accident. The reaction was a wake-up call. But it rang a bell in Hong Kong, not at all like the play-it-safe message it would have carried in Hollywood. Certainly Chan had become uninsurable. Yet the incident gave him automatic, unimpeachable Number One International Daredevil status, adding a new dimension of danger to the cult of personality that surrounded him.

In *Project A*, Jackie (above right on table) plays a Marine Corps sergeant who teams up with a policeman and a crook to fight the most notorious pirate of the South China Sea. The film grossed 14 million Hong Kong dollars in its first week of release and helped firmly establish the pattern of action and comedy that would become Jackie's trademark.

Looking Death in the Face

Chan had taken it as the duty of his stardom to court and reward the love of his fans by giving all of his energies and talents to his movies. Now it seemed a possibility that he might, through what David Chute calls a "masochistic fetish for authenticity," someday give his life. It also seemed a possibility that the star's emergence as a very good director might get lost, as Chan became his own most astounding special effect. Between then and now, there have been more than a dozen years, many broken bones for Jackie Chan, and one very close call (his forty-five-foot header onto rocks while shooting *Armor of God* in Yugoslavia in 1986). Yet only a few months ago, *New Yorker* writer Fredric Dannen quoted the superstar's enduring self-description: "Everybody knows Jackie Chan is crazy."

After the hearty reception of *Project A*, Chan told one martial arts journalist that he'd like not to direct for a few years. He said he wanted instead to work on his English, to learn tap dancing, and most of all to study acting seriously. But starring roles in *Winners and Sinners* (1983) and the other Sammo Hung–directed ensemble comedies that soon followed apparently pointed the way to Chan's playing his underdog/overachiever persona as a contemporary Hong Kong policeman.

Chan kept going with the lovable and gutsy qualities of his *Project A* character when he returned to directing in 1985 with *Police Story* (1985). And box-office results for this all-out action comedy entirely justified his having put a portion of those Dustin Hoffman dreams on hold to play a modern big-city cop—pretty much as himself. "I am always the same," he later told David Chute. "What you see here and what's on the screen, there's no difference." With slight modifications to the personality on offer, Chan was destined to direct himself in four more pictures, involving three different concept franchises (series of movies): *Project A II*, *Police Story II*, and the *Indiana Jones* takeoffs—*Armor of God* and *Armor of God II*—within the next six years.

When Chan talked with *Inside Kung-Fu* late in 1986, he was justly proud of the realism of the fight action and the raw energy of the stuntwork in Hong Kong films, as well as of his own smooth mid-1980s transition to action movies. By doing what came naturally and using what came easily to hand, Chan had effortlessly repeated and reversed the age-old Chinese gambit of turning objects of common use into weapons of war: tables and chairs, instead of traditional Chinese weapons, and cars, motorcycles, and bicycles. He listed a mere sampling of the "action aids" deployed in *Police Story*, *The Protector* (1984), and *Project A*. What he didn't have to do, he explained, was return to the lockstep fight stylings of most films of the 1970s. But, he said, "I do have to make action movies. Those are my trademark. My expertise lies with action films—Jackie Chan–style."

"Jackie Chan–Style" Action

What is a "Jackie Chan–style" action film? Several stateside commentators have understood that it's unlike the story-formulaic Hollywood action film of today. It's a mix of wild physical comedy with spectacular stunts, of slapstick and dynamite sticks. Some Chan fans think of the varied elements as colorful bits inside a kaleidoscope that Jackie's directorial hand has to turn just so, to reveal the final brilliant and amazing design of a movie.

Richard Corliss is among the well-known reviewers who have seen that the "Jackie Chan film" stands without current competition in giving the action back to the actor and, thereby, the action movie back to the moviegoer. And ironically, Chan starts where American moviemakers used to start, back when our first moving pictures were about "pictures that move" with the action elements. "I'm always trying to imagine funny and dangerous stunts," the filmmaker told *MAMA* fanzine writer Caroline Vie. "I always think of the stunts first and of how many I'll be able to put in the film."

Described by some as the "quintessential Jackie Chan film," *Project A* gave Jackie full reign to display his flair for physical comedy as well as the opportunity to work with his old boyhood chums, Sammo Hung and Yuen Biao.

Whereas for his earliest self-directed pictures he began by hiring a team of writers to find story pretexts for the several fight scenes he desired, Chan now plays out that process with regard to stunts. And during production Chan will now use everyone from an assistant prop person to a director to bring him objects, thus feeding him fresh ideas for action gags. But with the variety of stunts possible in a real-world setting—on the water and in the air, as well as on solid ground—contemporary pictures are, as Internet user Allan Wong reported Chan's telling a 1994 Vancouver Film Festival audience, more perilous to make than his earlier films.

At that appearance and elsewhere, Chan admitted he's afraid to do some of the stunts, but is urged into action when the moment comes for the cameras to roll. The characters he's played have never been totally intrepid. Neither is Jackie himself. Some of his motivation for risking all shows in Chan's words to David Chute: "I knew I had to be different. I always wanted to do something nobody else can do. With special effects, anybody can be Superman. But nobody else can be Jackie Chan." To Richard Corliss also, Chan spoke of being able to do "a lot of things that normal people can't do."

But American onlookers make little of all the death-defying when they award gold stars to Chan. Chan twice modified Hong Kong martial arts movies, first by

Jackie Chan, the man whom Kevin Thomas of the *L. A. Times* once referred to as "a one-man Cirque du Soleil."

becoming the raison d'être of late 1970s–early 1980s kung fu comedies, then by blending this new wrinkle with a larger scope and bigger action sequences more comically exotic than those seen in action movies anywhere before. If Chan's skin-stripping slide down the string of live lights in *Police Story* brought back the little swing that Arnold Schwarzenegger's stunt double took in the galleria scene of *Commando* (1985), it was an echo louder in duration and energy level than the original. Much more often, Chan leads the way. As Manohla Dargis puts it in *L.A. Weekly*, "Nearly a decade before James Cameron had actors hanging off flying machines in *True Lies* (courtesy of blue screens, mind you), Asia's answer to Arnold was swinging off a hot-air balloon in *Armor of God*." Chan's action freestyling obviously "translates," and travels well around the globe.

Sylvester Stallone has said that his friend Jackie is in good part responsible for the longevity of action pictures here and abroad, for extending the lifetime of "a genre that has grown pretty stale. He's infused films with humor and character-driven story while giving audiences these extraordinary stunts that are unparalleled anywhere in the world." Stallone is only one of the Chan supporters respected by the film community.

Just as much as *Police Story* laid waste to an entire Hong Kong shantytown, it built up for Chan an even larger following of American cult fans and then, with its exposure at the 1987 New York Film Festival, grew him a loose nationwide coterie of film-critic champions. In the intervening years, the word on Chan has spread significantly via the establishment press. In the *L.A. Times*, Kevin Thomas calls him "a one-man Cirque du Soleil." *Time* magazine's Richard Corliss praises the breadth of his talents and describes him as having mastered the best of what the silent movie clowns had to teach, "the universal language of film: action and passion, humor and heart." Along with the rest of them, the *New York Daily News*'s Dave Kehr marvels at his "physical self-possession."

They're going on about Chan's imagination and his physical virtuosity, not necessarily his defiance of death. A new audience awaits here, one that's somewhat inured to filmic extremes through overexposure to special effects—one that can probably learn to love Jackie Chan not least for his mind.

—Jean Ferguson

Abbreviations

Meaning of Abbreviations Used in the Text

Since many of Jackie Chan's interviews have already been published by CFW Enterprises in various magazine articles, the editor decided not to include the specific page numbers for the extracts in this book. However, reference sources appear at the end of each extract. Unless otherwise indicated, all questions and answers featured in this book are taken from John Little's interview with Jackie Chan recorded on February 3, 1998, and excerpted in *Inside Kung-Fu* magazine.

Abbreviation	Article Title	Magazine	Author/Interviewer	Date
IJC	"Inside Jackie Chan"	*Inside Kung-Fu*	James Lew/Paul Maslak	October 1980
JC/10GS	"Jackie Chan's Ten Greatest Stunts"	*Martial Arts Legends*	Dr. Craig D. Reid	April 1997
JC/PNP	"Jackie Chan— Pulling No Punches"	*Martial Arts Legends*	Mike Leeder	April 1997
SS	"Star Story"	*Martial Arts Movies*	Jean Ferguson	February 1996
UC	"Uncompromising Jackie"	*Inside Kung-Fu*	Dr. Craig D. Reid	March 1994

On Childhood

The Hong Kong hospital where Jackie Chan made his first appearance still stands in what is otherwise a much-changed city. Born Chan Kong Sang (literally "born in Hong Kong"), young Chan weighed in at a whopping twelve pounds! His parents lived in Victoria Peak and were so poor that they considered selling him to the doctor who delivered him. His father was a cook at the French embassy and his mother worked there as a housekeeper.

When Jackie was just six years old, his parents were offered work at the American embassy in Canberra, Australia. They had little money to raise their children and wanted Jackie to have a Chinese education. So when Sifu ("teacher") Yu Chan Yuen offered to pay Chan's parents a small sum to enroll their son in the school of his Chinese Opera Research Institute (the Hong Kong equivalent of the Peking opera school), they accepted and enrolled their then-seven-year-old son, and left him in Hong Kong.

Enrollment in the opera school meant acceptance of its almost unbelievably strict rules. Disobedience would be punished severely. But Jackie couldn't leave. His parents had enrolled him for the maximum time—ten years—no matter how bad the treatment, and there was no place to which he could run away. His parents were thousands of miles away in Australia.

The aim of the school was to turn out performers for the age-old, highly stylized, highly disciplined art form of China that is Peking Opera. A Chinese opera troop is more like a circus or magic show in the Western context. For Jackie it meant ten years of daily work at mastering acrobatics, acting, mime, and kung fu, for the purpose of performing tales of Chinese legend. While with the opera,

Jackie traveled all over Southeast Asia and appeared as a child actor in a number of movies.

When were you born, Jackie?

April 7th, 1954.

Is that a good day?

[Laughing] Better than April the first.

How did you come to acquire your English name of Jackie Chan?

It's kind of a long story, but because I was such a large, fat baby, I was given the Chinese nickname A-Puo, which means "cannonball." Then, at age six, when I moved to Australia, my schoolteacher thought I said, "Paul." But, because I couldn't pronounce "Paul" well enough, I was called "Steve." When I worked on a construction site, my friend thought "Steve" was no good, so he introduced me as "Jack Chan." I added on the "Y" because "Jacky" has a better rhythm. Then Raymond Chow[1] changed my name to "Jackie." (UC)

How exactly did you come to be enrolled in the Chinese opera school?

My parents immigrated to Australia when I was very young, but they wanted me to study in a Chinese school. So one of my father's friends suggested that since I was so active, I should be sent to an opera school. The discipline there is like at a military school, or a reform school, and my family went to Australia. (IJC)

How old were you then?

I was seven-and-a-half years old. (IJC)

Is that where you first got involved with the martial arts?

Yes, in the Northern styles of kung fu. (IJC)

Who was your kung-fu master?

Well, Yu Chan Yuen was the master of the opera school. But I trained with a lot of different teachers. Someone would teach me knives, someone would teach me somersaults. But I can't remember all of their names [laughing]—I don't want to because I hated their guts! They were always so hard on us, so I can't remember their names. (IJC)

Could you tell us just what exactly is an opera school?

Well, it's a pretty unique thing. It's more or less like when you join a circus or something. You have to sign a contract. In my case, I was committed for ten years. Then they train you in this school. You live there. Your parents pay tuition, and they provide you with room and board. They train you in different types of martial arts, acrobatics, and the Peking Opera. Also, they educate you there. A tutor would spend two or three hours a day teaching you Chinese literature. The school was a whole world in itself. You ate, slept, and practiced there. (IJC)

Was there any other formal education besides Chinese literature?

When it came to academics, my fellow students and I weren't that interested. While I was at the school, they had to replace eleven academics instructors because we used to beat the hell out of them. You see, we *really*

Jackie had all the money and all the time in the world to make *Dragon Lord* (below), which was supposed to be a follow-up to his film, *The Young Master.* The film remains important because it contains what many critics maintain is the finest scene of "street" kung-fu fighting ever done.

weren't into academics at all. Our main course of study was Chinese literature, but we were also taught English and arithmetic. A teacher was hired for each subject. Nothing was taught in great detail, just a mixture of a little bit of everything. It was very much like private tutoring. Unfortunately, the teachers got chased out of the school all the time because we didn't like to sit down and learn to read and write. We wanted to jump up and down and practice the martial arts. So we hated the academics teachers. It was like a little blackboard jungle. I mean, here we were studying kung fu, so we all ganged up on the teachers so that they'd quit, right? Like if you walked into a classroom of disobedient students, didn't make much money, and they beat up on you, you'd quit too, wouldn't you? (IJC)

Yes. Yes, I would. Didn't they discipline you?

The master would hit us. But he wasn't always around. (IJC)

What was the worst thing that happened to you as child with the opera?

Well, when I was ten or eleven, we were doing a performance in honor of an ancient grandmaster. I was sort of fooling around on stage before a live audience. The master was furious. He wanted to punish me right then and there—100 strikes of the rod! The audience started to plead on my behalf to reduce the punishment to fifty strikes. Anyway, after the show ended, the rattan stick, a long bench—and I—were brought out. (IJC)

That must have been rather embarrassing.

It hurt more. Then there was another time, when I was a kid, we had to practice standing on our heads for an hour at a time. I cheated by leaning on a table when the master was not looking. The other students and I must have leaned on that table too often because it collapsed on me, and I dislocated my finger. The master attended to my finger but gave me ten strokes of the rod afterwards. I couldn't train for a month. And even when it healed, I still claimed that it hurt because I was having too good a time watching the others work out hard. As a rule, at the school, you didn't tell the master that you were sick. Otherwise, he'd tell everybody to take a rest for the remainder of the day and only you would train! He'd have you do all kinds of strenuous exercises to make you sweat and perspire and get rid of the fever. So if you were really sick, you pretended that you were not. (IJC)

"By midnight, I was so exhausted that I didn't even take off my shoes."—Jackie Chan, on his early days in the Chinese Opera Research Institute

Was there anything that you liked about that school?

Well, the boys and the girls got to sleep together. Unfortunately, we *all* got to sleep together—there was this big rug that we slept on. It was old and dirty. Man had pissed on it, dog had pissed on it. I mean it was really filthy. Anyway, we slept with our shoes on because we didn't have time to take them off. We woke up every morning at five o'clock and cheated on our headstands until the maids warned us about the masters' approach. At ten o'clock we'd have breakfast—only one roll per person. We hated the period between ten and twelve o'clock the most—that's when we had to train our legs. The exercises were extremely painful. After lunchtime was weapons practice. And after dinner was academics—another time we hated. Then, after all of that was over, and everyone was sleepy, we had to sit and let the master point out everybody's progress. By midnight, I was so exhausted that I didn't even take off my shoes. (IJC)

How many days a week did that go on?

Sunday was the [only] day off, but because my parents were in Australia I didn't get to go home like the others. I would have to stay, sleep on the floor, and clean up the place. (IJC)

Did you see a lot of bad things, violence, growing up in Hong Kong?

When I was young, yes. I saw people get killed, I saw people selling drugs—all those bad things. It's not that my life was really bad, but it was bad.

At an early age, Jackie had seen enough, and decided that he wanted to become something far better than the drugsellers and criminals that he saw growing up in Hong Kong.

It's obvious that at this young age you decided that this was not what you wanted to do with your life. What was it at that age that you think created your ambition to become something better than the drugsellers and criminals you saw?

I always remembered something that my father told me. Around me at that time were all the triads (Chinese organized-crime "families"). And in the old days, all of the triad organizations tried to recruit me for their gangs. "Come, come, come," they'd say to me. But I remember my father saying, "Never get in the triads—and no drugs." Those two things I promised my father. I said, "OK." And then my father left me and went back to Australia and I was left by myself in Hong Kong. And ever since then I've stayed away from the triads. Even if a friend of mine was in the triads, I would tell him to go away from me. He was OK—he was still my friend until he did something wrong. If he sold drugs, I would just go away. We'd sit at the same table—until the drugs came out.

It's hard, I think, for people in America and around the world to understand just how prevalent the triads are in Hong Kong. But they've been there for decades—centuries, in fact, which must have made it especially hard for you growing up to do what your father told you to do when the triad influence was everywhere. How were you able to do that without offending the leaders of these triads and putting your own life at risk?

I just pretended to be dumb to their requests and, also, I was quite young at that time. I'm quite lucky. I pretended that I didn't know anything and they would just say, "Oh, leave him alone." And also, my personality has always been happy-go-lucky—ha, ha, ha, hee, hee, hee. They just treated me like a very good friend and were just waiting, I think, until I got a little bit older, and maybe then I would need their help, or something like that—which, of course, is how they trap you. Also, at this point I developed an interest in bowling.

How would bowling serve as a preventive measure to the triads?

Well, suddenly I was not going to the pool halls any more, where a lot of the triad members would congregate. You see, there were a lot of British-owned pool halls in Hong Kong at that time, and until I discovered bowling I would hang out in the pool halls quite a bit—even sleep in the pool halls. I liked the pool halls because there was always something exciting going on in there. At that time our schools didn't have basketball, or soccer—we had nothing. When I first got out of the opera everything was new to me—there was a whole new world out there! I learned that I liked soccer very much, then three months later I learned and liked boxing. After boxing I learned that there was gambling going on, so then I liked gambling. After gambling there was pool, and I continued to play pool—people were always introducing me to new things. And I loved pool, I would play it almost twenty-four hours a day. And, while I was not professional, I became very, very good at it—a champion, in fact. You know, young people always learn things very quickly, so I learned pool until some people said, "We're going to play bowling." Then I found out that I liked bowling, and so I'd spend up to twenty-four hours a day playing bowling. But bowling is different. A bowling alley is very big. Sometimes I would go to the bowling alley and sleep—just by myself. So the bowling alley helped me in a way to get away from the triads. The triads are not usually found hanging around in bowling alleys.

On Martial Arts and Fighting

lthough Jackie Chan is considered first and foremost an "action star" by the vast majority of his fans and film critics, his expertise and mastery of the martial arts cannot be denied. And, given that he has studied multiple arts, his insights are deeper and more varied than most "masters" and "experts," who devote themselves solely to one art for their entire lives. Jackie also is able to separate the functional and practical from the purely ornate. He grew up on the mean streets of Hong Kong, and was—as you shall read—involved in altercations that had very serious consequences.

While Jackie downplays his fighting skills, often telling reporters that "anybody can beat me up," such self-effacing comments should be taken as an expression of his sense of humor. Jackie Chan is a well-schooled martial artist who has trained himself in many diverse forms of combat (both unarmed and armed) and who is in peak physical condition. These elements taken together result in a very powerful, fast, and lethal human being and an expert martial artist by any standard you would care to use.

Do you consider yourself an expert in all facets of the martial arts?

Right now, because I'm not training as intensively in the martial arts as I did before, I would not call myself a "martial arts expert." Before, I might have said that I was a martial arts expert, because I was actively training in many different martial arts. I learned Southern-style kung fu, Northern-style kung fu, hapkido, judo—everything. But after I started doing movies, I just mixed it all in together. Now if you asked me, "Jackie, do the Bak Mei," I already have forgotten the routine! I only remember a part of it because I have mixed in so many martial arts into my training over the years for the movies. Right now I would consider myself an expert in martial arts in the movies.

I wanted to touch on your martial arts background. You've said that you studied all sorts of different martial arts, so what would you consider your "style" of martial art?

"I know all the different styles [of martial art] . . . but right now I can't say that my style is any one of them. I'm like a 'chop-suey expert.' You name it, I know it."—Jackie Chan

Right now it's "chop suey." [laughs] I mean, I know all the different styles; I can talk to you about judo, tae kwon do—I know everything, but right now I can't say that my style is any one of them. I'm like a "chop-suey expert." You name it, I know it. In each individual art I am not an expert, but on the whole thing, I'm the expert. And if you are talking about fighting for a movie, I'm the big expert.

When you first started martial arts training in the Peking Opera, what was the style they trained you in?

It was a Northern style. It dealt with everything. After the Northern style, I learned the Southern style. And after the Southern style, I learned the Bak Mei ("white eyebrow") style. I concentrated quite heavily on the white eyebrow style.[2]

What are your thoughts on all of the various styles you've studied in the martial arts?

Actually, all the styles are almost the same, only the titles are different. I was really interested in learning other martial arts after I learned the styles I just mentioned, so I went on and studied some other arts after these. I went on to learn hapkido for six months, tae kwon do, judo, Wing Chung for three months, boxing for another six months, and I learned that only boxing was different. Boxing's punches are different, but these other martial arts are almost the same. Hapkido, tae kwon do, karate—the same! They're just a little different in some small respects. Then I found out—because I'm crazy about martial arts—that it's only their titles that are different. Every art's the same. Right now if I opened a school, I could call it "Dragon Do." Then after somebody learned from me, say, Curtis Wong, he could call it "Dragon Curtis Do." Right now there are just too many arts with names like Jak Koo Soo, Su Chi Soo, Ha Soo Soo—too many things going on—but the basic things are all the same. They just change some things a little bit, like, Wing Chun puts the hand out like this, Bak Mei puts the hand out with a

Jackie believes that all styles of martial arts are essentially the same and that their differences lie only in their respective titles.

slightly different arc, Hung Kune does it similarly— all they've done is called what they do by different names, but basically it's the same thing. Like a gun and a bullet—pow! But now they have machine guns, revolvers, semiautomatics, but they're still guns. Just a little bit different.

Going back in your past for a moment, have you ever had to use your martial arts for real? Have you ever had a real fight?

Yes. When I was young.

Really? Can you remember the details of it?

You know, the thing is that when you learn a martial art and then you have a fight in the street, you usually end up using only a certain part of your martial art training. And that's usually just what comes to you naturally—"bam! bam! bam!" A real fight is rather wild and uncontrolled—not like you see in the movies where a guy will do fifteen blocks

According to Jackie, "A real fight is rather wild and uncontrolled—not like you see in the movies where a guy will do fifteen blocks and end up in a stance."

and end up in a stance. But at that moment, when you're fighting, you're really fast. In the fight you are asking about, I was one of three people who ended up in a fight against six people. They all went down and I, myself, got hurt. I ran away afterwards and when I was running away I heard my shoes—at that time we didn't have "airshoes," we just had the Chinese slipper type of shoes—and they were sloshing against the ground as I ran. Then I looked down at my shoe, and it was all soaked with blood! Then I went to the store, called White Stone, and I changed my jeans and—do you know Hong Kong?

I was there once.

Well, I crossed the street to look back at where the fight was and I saw that the police had come, the ambulance had also come [laughs]—yeah! Just once. It was a big fight on the street. Then I had other fights at the school with Sammo [Hung][3] and some other brothers.[4] Yeah, we used to fight a lot.

The one where the ambulance and the police came—what happened afterward?

I don't know what happened. I just saw a lot of people standing around.

How did you feel after the fight?

Well, for twenty or thirty seconds immediately after the fight, you just tremble and shake. I ran away, and even when I was talking to my friends I was shaking. You just can't help it. My whole hand was shaking and hurt. I found that a bone in my hand had popped up through the skin and I tried to push it down but I couldn't. Then I saw a white thing in my knuckle showing through the skin and I tried again to push it back inside my knuckle, but I couldn't do it. Later on, however, it just popped out! I thought, "What was that?" It turned out to be the other guy's tooth—from his mouth. I think it went into my knuckle when I threw a backfist at him. I hurt for two weeks after the fight, and my muscles were sore. My whole body ached, and yet the fight was like—wham! bam! bam! wham!—it was over so fast.

How old were you when this happened?

Oh, like, seventeen years old.

Do you remember how it started?

Yeah, just by looking. There were six people standing next to their motorcycles. The motorcycles were standing up, all of them right beside each other. Then we were passing by and I said, "Ahh, my dream is to one day have a motorcycle!" I just pointed at them. And one of the guys turned around— and this was at night—and said, "What the f*** are you pointing at?" Then I said, "Oh-oh!" Then my friend went over and, with one kick, knocked all six of the motorcycles down. Then he ran over to fight with these guys. Then my other friend, who was still standing next to me, ran over to fight—except me. Then I looked at myself and thought, "What am I doing standing here?" Then I went over and started fighting—"boom! boom! boom!"—and that was it. Just that quick.

And that was the point at which you took off running with your bloody shoe?

Yeah. We all got hurt. You just don't know what's going on in a situation like that. Boom! Boom! Boom! It was over so fast. Do you remember Yuen Kwei? One of my brothers [from the opera] is a director right now, named Yuen Kwei. And I remember feeling so excited afterwards, thinking, "Wow, I can fight so good!" Then I stayed in Tsim Sha Tsui. I sat down on the side of the road with Yuen Kwei. There were, like, four people walking by and they said in Cantonese, "Hey, you Japanese!" Yeah, they called me Japanese, so I turned around and, acting tough, said, "Screw you!" Then these four people just stopped and stared at me and I said, "What the hell are you looking at?" Then they ran away. Then Yuen Kwei turned to me and said, "Jackie, be careful." And I said, "Oh, what the hell."

And then, a few days later, [laughs] now here's a long story: there's me, my bigger brother, and another bigger brother—we're three people—and we were going to Yuen Biao's place to play mah-jongg. We walk, walk, walk toward his apartment. We had to pass a park to get to the entrance to his apartment, and I noticed that there were six people standing around in the

> "When you learn a martial art and then you have a fight in the street, you usually end up using only a certain part of your martial art training. And that's usually just what comes to you naturally—'bam! bam! bam!'"—Jackie Chan

park. So I looked at my two bigger brothers and said, "Hey, there are only six people—you think we can knock them down?" We all thought, "Yes, let's go!" Then we went to each of them, one by one, and gave each one of them a really tough look to see if they wanted to fight. [laughs] We walk, walk, walk and the six people just stood there watching us. We gave them the look—nothing. So we felt pretty tough and went on to Yuen Biao's place to play mah-jongg. After about thirty minutes, we heard these voices from outside: "F*** you! Aaaagh!" We turned around and there were at least fifty people with knives! "Come on out!" [laughs] We thought, "Shit!" But we just turned around and continued playing mah-jongg, hoping they would go away.

The doors in Hong Kong—fortunately for us—had a type of iron gate or iron door that you could see through in front of the main door. They were still yelling at us, "Come out! Come out now—the whole building is surrounded!" Then, Yuen Kwei and I decided that we had better go out. One of my bigger brothers picked up two barbecue forks and gave them to us for weapons. I put mine inside my sleeve thinking if something went wrong outside, I'd pull it out and use it. But, realistically, what could I do? If I had to fight, I would have had no choice! So one of their guys comes up to me and says, "Where are you from?"—they were talking in Chinese slang, like, from the triads. "Where are you from? You have something in your pocket?" The "pocket" means "Where are you from?"—that kind of slang. I tried to not understand and play dumb. I said, "What are you talking about my *pocket*? I have nothing." He said, "F*** you! Don't try to play dumb! You know what I'm talking about!" I said, "No, I don't. I'm in the film business." He said, "The film business? Do you know somebody?" I said, "*Know* his name? No." He was getting madder at this point, so I said, "Ah, sorry, maybe I would remember his face, because most of the time I call him by his name in the movie, so I don't know his real name." Then he got even more mad and said, "Why were you looking at us?" And I said, "Because I wanted to ask where the place was we were supposed to go to. And then later on we decided not to ask and that we'd just go look around for it ourselves." So, he went on and on and then finally said, "OK, you two can go." [laughs]

Those were the "tough old days." And while all this was going on, people were coming up and yelling, "Don't talk—kill him!" So we were just standing there, scared to death, and the guy says, "OK, now you have to say sorry to my big brother." Then a young boy came up—they wanted to play with us—this young boy comes up and I had to bow my head and say, "Sorry, sorry, sorry." And then they said, "OK—nothing! Remember, this is *our* territory! Just because you have a friend who stays here doesn't mean you're safe!" And then they split.

You know what? After we walked down the stairs from all of this, those six people were still there standing in the park. They looked right at us and just smiled. So we walked, walked, walked. We could have just gone home, you know? But for some reason, I felt that we had to walk around these same six people again! I don't know, we were trying to be brave or something. This time, however, there was no looking at them—nothing too scary. Then we walked way past them and were standing there. I don't know what my brothers were thinking, but I was thinking, "Come on, taxi, hurry up and get here!" And then the taxi pulled up, and we were very quiet and subdued at this point. I remember thinking that I kept hearing footsteps running up behind us. Anyway, the taxi finally arrived, I opened the door, got in the cab, closed the door—still looking out the window and behind us for the gang. As soon as the taxi began to drive away, all three of us rolled down the windows of the taxi and yelled, "You want a fight? Come on, you cowards!!" [laughs] What could we do—except hope that the taxi wouldn't stop! That was the last time I had any trouble like that.

That must have been quite an introduction to life—as it really is on the streets of Hong Kong—as compared to how it was in a Peking Opera school.

Right, because we didn't know any better. We were in a school, protected from the realities of the outside world by our master. Wherever I went in school, there were always thirty or forty people surrounding me. Suddenly to come out—like a bird leaving its parents and nest—to fly wherever I wanted, I quickly discovered that there were a lot of hungry eagles out there. Until that time, we thought we were the best fighters. But out on the street we learned that people don't fight that way; if you fight two people, they'll come back with four people; if you come with four people, they'll come back with ten people. Then we learned that, "Wow, society is really that bad." They're not coming to fight with fists only, they're coming with knives and, if you take their knives away, they'll bring a gun, and if you take their gun away, then they'll come back at you with a machine gun! That's when I understood that I had to be careful out there. And now I just keep as far away from trouble as I can. I just keep away from it.

Hong Kong street gangs were supposed to be really vicious back then.

Yeah, in the old days. Yes. I think it's the same everywhere, though. Even now, whenever I travel, people say "don't go to this place" or "don't go to that place" because of the street gangs. There are bad areas all over the world, and so they take me away from there. I always stay away from places where there's trouble. I always stay in a good area. It's kind of like the old days again, in that I've kind of forgotten what the bad things are now. So I always see the good things and, although I've seen plenty of bad things in my life, I don't want to glorify that in my movies. So that's why when I made *Rumble in the Bronx*, I didn't want to make the Bronx area a really, really dark or ugly place, so I made the Bronx more pretty and more happy-go-lucky.

Jackie's intensive training of more than 30 years in the martial arts has given him a very broad insight and expertise. "You name it, I know it," he says.

On Health and Fitness

It would be calling attention to the obvious to say that Jackie Chan is in incredible shape. The muscles that adorn the Chan physique not only ripple and look impressive, but they are also highly functional. They have to be, for Jackie Chan is not in the business of "second chances." His stunts are very—very—unforgiving. If his strength, endurance, and suppleness aren't the best he is capable of—at all times—he is inviting disaster.

Over the years people have attempted to pin Jackie down as to just how he keeps in such fantastic shape, and how he builds the strength, stamina, and flexibility necessary to do the spectacular fight scenes and amazing stunts that have continued to dazzle audiences around the world over the past two decades. Now you are about to find out.

Jackie, you are obviously in excellent shape. What do you do to keep in shape?

There was a time that I used to run forty-five minutes every day, but after *Rumble in the Bronx* I broke my ankle. Now, after I run fifteen to twenty minutes, my ankle really starts to hurt. And also after I filmed the Mountain Dew commercials, my left ankle and knee also developed some problems. So right now I'm doing the Master Step [stairclimber exercise machine] for one hour every other day. On Mondays, for example, I'll do one hour, and then I'll not do the Master Step on Tuesday. I'll come back in and do it again on Wednesday, take Thursday off, and then do it again on Friday and take Saturday off—and so on.

At what level do you set the Master Step? Is it at an intense level?

No, at a normal level. I can't go too low or too high because of the ankle and the knee. I try to keep it as flat as possible. Even sometimes when I don't have access to a Master Step, I will walk on the street, but on a flat surface. The best is the grass because it is soft and absorbs the impact better. I'll do this for one hour.

Do you do any weight training?

Yes, usually after working out on the Master Step, I'll do some light weight training. I use very simple movements like dumbbell laterals, dumbbell flyes, bench presses—that type of thing. I don't use heavy weights.

What kind of weight would you use, for example, on the bench-press exercise?

I'd use about forty-five kilos [100 pounds] on each side.

And for how many repetitions?

Twenty or thirty—done at a very quick pace.

How many sets of each exercise would you perform?

I average around four sets per exercise.

Do you work out training different body parts on different days?

No, I just work out depending on how I feel like it, because I have very good basic martial arts training that I do with my stuntmen, so we really don't need to train different body parts on any type of schedule. When you're on a set, when we are fighting, there is already a lot of movement and exercise from the choreography we do. Plus, we just don't want to get too big—especially on our shoulders and arms.

Your shoulders and arms are very well developed for someone who doesn't do a lot of specialized weight training for them. Is this muscle development a result of your martial arts training?

Yeah, I think when I was younger.

And gymnastics?

Yeah, gymnastics is very good for strength, and when you do things like flips and hanging upside-down, it also helps you with your coordination.

You have a very good sense of body awareness. By that I mean a great sense of balance and coordination. Is that something you can train for—or is it simply a genetic factor?

No, you can definitely train for it. The most important thing is to train for it when you are young. When I was six-and-a-half or seven years old, at that time we had a very good basic training. It didn't matter how we felt—we had to do push-ups, knee bends, and so on. The basic training is very important. After all those years it becomes very natural. It's actually very hard to tell you how I train, because I just "know" what to do. When I lose my balance, I just know how to get it back. So, this way, when I do

Jackie credits his early gymnastics training for giving him a great base of strength, body awareness, and coordination—not to mention muscularity!

a stunt, I do get hurt sometimes, but less than some other people.

Because of your conditioning.

Right.

You mentioned that you do bench presses, dumbbell laterals for your shoulders, dumbbell flyes for your chest. Do you do any weight training for your legs?

No, just kicking. I do kicking and punching exercises.

How do you train in this fashion? How many days would you perform punching and kicking exercises?

Every other day. Every other day is hard training, like, really kicking and punching hard. Some other days it's like fooling around—[begins to punch at the air] boom! boom! boom! boom! boom! kick! kick! kick! kick! kick!— just depending upon how we feel on any given day. Some days we just lie

According to Jackie, "It's actually very hard to tell you how I train, because I just 'know' what to do. When I lose my balance, I just know how to get it back."

down, we just don't want to do it. Some other days we are really kicking and punching hard for three minutes every round, then take thirty seconds rest, then another three minutes of punching, followed by another thirty seconds rest, followed by another three minutes. You just keep on punching—boom! boom! boom! boom! boom!—until your three minutes are up, no matter how slow or tired you get. You just finish up for three minutes, then you rest another thirty seconds.

So do you mix it up—that is, three minutes of punching, thirty seconds rest; three minutes of kicking, thirty seconds rest; and so on in this fashion—or do you combine punching and kicking for three-minute intervals followed by thirty seconds rest?

No, it's punch first—punch, punch, punch, then kick, kick, kick. Then punching/kicking, punching/kicking.

And are the punches and kicks of any type (that is, random combinations and techniques), or do you practice only certain kicks and punches for training purposes?

No, they are of any type. Because we already have a solid basic training, the most important thing is to keep flexible and to keep the movements fluid.

So what do you train your kicks on—an air shield, a heavy bag?

A bag. I use a standing bag.[5]

How long would all of this take—that is, to complete all of your three-minute intervals of punching and kicking—a half hour?

Yeah, more than a half hour.

This would also be excellent cardiovascular exercise, too, wouldn't it? After all, it gets your heart beating faster, your metabolism would increase....

Oh, yes.

Jackie has to be in top shape for each film as the script often calls for him to square off against world martial art champions, such as he did with real-life World Kickboxing Champion Benny "the Jet" Urquidez in this scene from *Wheels on Meals.*

Let me also ask you this. You say you used to run—now you step or walk and do your punching and kicking for cardiovascular fitness; you lift weights for strength fitness, but what do you do for flexibility? Do you stretch? What do you do to keep limber, to kick high and remain flexible?

When we're on the set, we just put our leg up on something and stretch. Even when we're talking, or if I'm having a conversation with my boys, everybody puts their leg up on a table, on a chair—we just put it up and stretch during conversations and breaks in between scenes.

Do you find any difference now in warming up, now that you're older, than when you first started in the industry?

Yes. Before, a long time ago, I didn't need to warm up, I'd just do it. But I've found out that it's very easy to twist my shoulder, hip, knee, and then I'm, like,

The muscularity of Jackie's chest, shoulders, and arms is the result of years of dedicated and intense training in gymnastics, martial arts, and progressive-resistance exercise.

"Aaagh!" Now, before I do a scene, all my boys make sure that all of us stretch, stretch, stretch. So now I stretch everything before I shoot a scene involving kicking and punching.

In movies such as **Rumble in the Bronx,** *where your physique is shown, do you have to engage in any different type of training, more specifically, bodybuilding or physique training, to acquire such a muscular appearance—or is this the kind of condition you are in all the time?*

No, I didn't need any specialized training. That's pretty much the condition I'm in almost all the time. Sometimes when I finish a movie, I'll travel around and, after one or two months off, I always think to myself, "I'm getting fat, I'm getting fat, I'm getting fat." Always in my mind. So then I know that I've got to start training again.

How long can you go before you feel you "have" to work out again?

After about two weeks to a month at the most, then I feel that I've got to work out.

What's your bodyweight right now?

72 kilos [158 pounds].

And how tall are you, approximately?

Five-ten-and-a-half.

How about your diet? What do you eat to keep so lean?

I really don't have a special diet. I eat everything. Of course, I watch out not to eat things that are too oily. Mostly I eat vegetables and once or twice a week I'll eat ice cream, but mostly I just stop myself from eating too much junk food.

What about alcohol—do you drink at all?

I do drink but I have to watch it. If I drink a lot today—I'm talking about red wine—then the next day I make myself Master Step for one hour! And when I drink red wine and almost get drunk, or then eat some ice cream, then, again, the next day I'll do the Master Step, but this time for one-and-a-half hours! It's like a punishment for myself. No matter what, whenever I eat the heavy foods or the desserts, I tell myself, "OK, that's another two minutes, another three minutes [of exercise]," depending upon what I eat. [laughs] Then the next day, when I'm doing this exercise, I'm thinking to myself—"Whew! Why am I doing all this work? Why did I eat all that food?" Then, at night, I have to be careful because somebody is always bringing me stuff to eat or drink that I shouldn't be having. Like, when I go out to a party, I'm like a target! Everybody's focus is on me and it's "Come on Jackie, let's have a toast!" And then as the evening wears on later and later, you forget or lose control of how much you've had to drink.

Part of Jackie's workout these days is a series of three-minute punching and kicking drills—performed for 30 minutes straight. You'd better believe that such intensive exercise will work up a sweat!

Red wine has been proven good for people in small doses. So do you like to have a little red wine every day?

Not every day, it depends.

What is your favorite type of red wine? Are you a connoisseur?

Because I started drinking red wine in Australia, it was very easy for me to learn. The first time I had red wine my English was not that good, so when I learned about red wine I didn't know about California wine, or French wine. Australian wine I find is very simple. The brand name is Grange—and that's it. And then they had numbers like Penfold 28, Penfold 407, Penfold 304—it was easy! Just number counting! So this way, I started with Australian wine. It was easy for me to remember. If a waiter came up to me in a restaurant, I didn't have to say "Chateau something," I'd just say, "Give me 28," or "Give me

37," or "Give me 407," "Give me a 389." They all count by the numbers, so it was easy for me to order that way.

As long as they don't bring you thirty-seven bottles of a particular wine, I suppose! [all laugh] Have you always been lean or muscular? You mentioned that sometimes you feel as though you are getting fat, but you must have a tremendous metabolism. Have you always been fairly muscular due to your years of training in gymnastics and martial arts?

I think so, yes. And also because I enjoy being active. I would rather walk than take the elevator. I don't want to take the escalator. If I can exercise, I'll do it. If there is an opportunity for exercise, I'll take it. For example, if I can walk up three flights of stairs, I'll walk up three flights of stairs, rather than taking an elevator. In life, I've found that most people these days are very lazy. Like, they will get in the elevator, then in their car, then, after their car ride, they get on the escalator, then sit down in the restaurant, then get back in their car for an hour's drive home; then when they get home they sit on their sofa, take hold of the remote control, then, within a half hour, they fall asleep. With such a lifestyle it's very easy to get fat! So mostly I make sure that I take the time to just walk, walk, walk, walk.

Jackie's first "American" film was *The Big Brawl,* which introduced Jackie's phenomenal physique and acrobatic martial arts to North American audiences for the first time.

Do you have an exercise machine in your house?

I do. Right now, yes.

Do you bring anything with you to help you keep in shape on the sets of your films when you travel?

Wherever I go around the world to film I just bring two pieces of exercise equipment with me: a barbell set and a bench press. That's all. Wherever I go, they break it down and pack it up. When I was recently filming in South Africa, they put it together in my room. I always have two rooms that interconnect when I travel, and one of those rooms is for exercising. I don't really use dumbbells and weights that much, however. Mostly these empty rooms are used more for practicing my punching and kicking. Punching, kicking, and jumping—these are more important than the dumbbells and the weights.

Although performed
primarily for comic
effect, this scene from
Drunken Master also
revealed Jackie's supreme
abdominal strength and
incredible body control.

On Philosophy

The martial arts are often referred to as a "spiritual discipline," in that they bestow upon their serious adherents some deep and lasting insights into the human condition. Most martial arts masters are themselves students of what we in the West call "the Queen of the Sciences," or as it is more popularly referred to, philosophy. Certainly Jackie Chan fits this mold. He possesses an extremely active mind, and it is obvious that he thinks about life—and how to live it—with as much passion and commitment as he thinks about his filmmaking. This is entirely fitting as how one builds one's character is at least as important as how one builds one's body or fashions a film. Fortunately, Jackie likes to combine his philosophy with his filmmaking, which makes his films watchable on many different levels. If you simply enjoy action, his films have enjoyment for you; if you enjoy comedy, then his films also are appealing; and if you enjoy films that express a message or contain a well-thought-out perspective on how we should live our lives to become better human beings, then his films hold a far deeper and redeeming meaning still.

There is a maxim that "figs do not sprout from thistles," and, similarly, good actions do not sprout from bad thoughts. To this end, you will learn from this chapter that Jackie Chan possesses not only an extremely healthy body (which you would expect, given his phenomenal acrobatic/athletic ability) but also a very healthy, positive mind.

In matters of ethics and religion, Jackie prefers to stand alone, trusting his heart—rather than the scriptures and rituals of organized theology.

Jackie, what is your philosophy of life?

I just like to look after myself and to improve. When I have time I try to engage in more training. Health is very important to me. And I also try to help other people. I help the elderly, I help the children who don't have a father or mother. I try to help people as often as possible because when I was young the Red Cross helped me quite a bit. I remember one time I went to thank the Father who worked there, and he said to me, "Don't thank me. When you grow up and you have more strength, then you can help some other people." So I think what I'm doing now is kind of like a payback to those people who helped me in the Red Cross.

What are your religious beliefs?

None. I don't have a religion. No religion at all. I just think you should trust more in your own heart. The more your own heart [is involved] the more the payback.

Did you read many of the Eastern philosophy books when you were growing up, such as the **Tao te Ching,** *the* **I Ching,** *or any of the Buddhist sutras?*

No. I just don't believe in those kinds of things. When I was young, yes, I believed. But I'm more grown-up now and I believe more in the things that I see. And what I see is that the thing that most people have died for is religion. All those years they kill each other over religious issues. So what are these religions good for? I don't think you should sit at home and tell the Buddha to help you have good health—no, *you* have to train and exercise, then you'll have good health! And also, the Buddha doesn't say that you *have* to believe in him. If he's in here [points to his heart], then I believe that he will always protect me. Why? Because I didn't kill anybody, I always help people. If there's a Buddha within, then he'll always be helping you.

You obviously feel the same way about the Western religious traditions, too.

Yes, [in these traditions] if you hit somebody or hurt somebody, then you go to the—what? The church?—useless! If you kill somebody you just go to the church and say, "Forgive me." If the God, or somebody else then forgives you, then I'm afraid that I don't like this kind of God.

What are your thoughts on God?

God is not Chinese or Japanese. If there is a God, then He helps everybody. I don't have to believe in Him. Even if I am in Hong Kong and God is in America, He has to protect me. God helps everybody. That's my philosophy. So I don't have to believe in Him. What I do is do the best that I can in the movie business. That helps me with survival. And a lot of other people are with me, I give them jobs. Secondly, if I earn some money, yes, I take care of my family, then I give to the charities. It makes me happy. That's all. So [among] all my boys, there is no "religion." No ghosts. No God. Nothing. We just try to help people. That's my philosophy.

What moves you in this respect? What makes you feel sad? I know you do a lot of work with underprivileged children to help them out, but I'm guessing that in Hong Kong, you are quite active with the hospitals. Do you help out in hospitals?

Yes, because later on in my career I found out that there were many children who watched my movies, so I made a conscious decision to cut down on my violence. If you look at my earlier films, my later films, and my present films, there is quite a difference in this respect. When you see *Drunken Master*, I was telling people they should mix drinking and fighting—this was wrong. There's too many children who watch my movies. How could I tell these children that drinking and fighting is OK? That's wrong! That movie was a comedy, but some children might take it seriously and it gave out the wrong message to these children. Then when *Drunken Master II* came out, I made sure that it gave out a different message: "Don't drink. Don't fight." It was far less violent, it contained no sex scenes, and it had no curse words in it. No blood. And my character was always happy-go-lucky, because I care about children. I know that children are watching my movies. It's very natural for me to care about children.

Jackie (right) often portrays police officers in his films, so he was particularly appreciative of receiving a San Francisco police officer's hat, presented to him by San Francisco Police Chief Fred Lau (left) just prior to the North American premiere of his film *First Strike*. Always the philanthropist, Jackie was in San Francisco to help raise money for the Self-Help for the Elderly's new Jackie Chan Center (located at 408 22nd Avenue in San Francisco).

In all of his films, Jackie makes sure that the audience knows that there are no "good" and "bad" races—only good and bad people. Here, he and partner Danny Aiello play two tough New York City policemen whose search for a kidnapped young woman embroils them in a dangerous world of international drug trafficking in *The Protector*.

What are your views, philosophically speaking, on issues such as racism? In America, there has long existed prejudice against different cultures and even against giving Asians leading roles in films. Even though you may be a big success and can come over and star in an American-made film, there are still not a lot of opportunities for Asians in the film business here in America. Has it been your experience that there is still a lot of racism here in America?

I think there is still a lot of racism in every country. In America, in Europe, in South Africa, even in Hong Kong—the Chinese call the Caucasian *gwei-lo* (foreign devil) and call the Chinese from China *Ah-Chan*.

What does that mean?

I don't know, it's kind of a term for a stupid person. They call similar names for the Vietnamese people. It's everywhere and I don't like it. I just don't like it. I think we should help everybody. Everybody should help everybody. That's why when I do charity work, it's not just for Hong Kong. When I do charity work, I'll do it in Malaysia, in Singapore, in Korea, in Taiwan, in China. I let them know that all the people in the whole world should be willing to look after each other. It helps to spread peace. Now there are already so many accidents going on, earthquakes, tornados—all kinds of problems to contend with already, so why do people have to fight against everybody? That's why when you look at my movies, like *Rumble in the Bronx* especially, there was a Chinese in the Bronx. Why? I did that on purpose. I let the audience know that the Chinese have good people—I'm the good person—but they also have bad people in the Bronx. Crime is not just something committed by black people or white people, it's also committed by Italians, French—and Chinese. So that way, it shows to the people who see my film that the world is full of good people and bad people of all races. No one race is good, and all the other races bad.

That's my philosophy. So when I'm making a movie, I have to put—even in *Who Am I?*—I put a Chinese guy in it and said, "Why do Chinese have to fight Chinese?" Unfortunately that scene was cut out because the movie was too long, but I will put it into one of my other movies with the hope that the Chinese government will see it. It's my way of saying, "China—don't fight Taipei; Taipei, don't fight China." That's my philosophy.

Then, of course, I put in a little comedy. I don't want to always be saying political things. I put a little politics in, and then I put in a little comedy. That's why when the bad guy is fighting me, I say, "Come on, why do the Chinese have to fight Chinese?" Then he says, "No, I don't hold a Chinese passport!" Then he starts fighting with me. Then, when I start to beat him up, he says, "No, no, no. I'm Chinese." And I say, "*Now* you say that you're Chinese!" You see, I put in a little politics with my comedy. I don't want to make movies like, say, some of the older Hong Kong films where the Chinese are always good and the *gwei-lo* are always bad. In my movie I want to put in that American people can help me and that they can also hurt me. Chinese people can help me but Chinese people can also hurt me. Everybody is the same. There's not only *one* way, there are *many* ways. That's my philosophy. Even when you see a Bruce Lee movie, in his first films, the Japanese are always the bad guys. He's this type of person, he's a big hero person [to the Chinese], but there's a lot of good Japanese, right? Even during World

"Everybody should help everybody. That's why when I do charity work, it's not just for Hong Kong. When I do charity work, I'll do it in Malaysia, in Singapore, in Korea, in Taiwan, in China. I let them know that all the people in the whole world should be willing to look after each other. It helps to spread peace."—Jackie Chan

War II. When he was making the American movies, then the Americans were always bad guys, and he was the good guy. I don't like that. I'm not this kind of person. When I make a movie in which there is a bad Japanese guy, then the people who are fighting with me and help me are also Japanese. That's my philosophy—just to let the people know, to tell the whole world, that even among your own people are bad people. Just don't promote something wrong. When you continue to make these kinds of movies, the children are made to think that "the Japanese are bad, bad, bad!" If that continues throughout his lifetime, he sees maybe 100 movies and thinks that all Japanese are bad. That's the wrong message. It's like the old education they used to have in Taipei—when you would open a history book you'd learn that the Japanese were nasty people. And whenever I would see a Japanese person I used to get scared.

You touched on education. Just how important is education in your opinion?

Education is very important. I do not have a very good education. What I learned I learned mainly from social interaction. I don't know how to read or write properly—even in Chinese. Of course, right now I can read a little bit. As far as writing goes, I have someone else write for me. As for English, I can talk a little bit, but I cannot read it or write it. So I want my second generation to have a very good education. Also, my father had no education, my mother had no education, no schooling. Me? No school. In this way I want my son to have a very good education. He can speak very good English and speak Mandarin, Cantonese. He can read Chinese, write Chinese. So, education is very important for everybody. If you have an education, then you know what's happened. You can judge good things from bad things.

Although you claim not to be educated, you speak something like five languages, don't you?

Not fluently, but I can speak a lot of languages. Like, I can speak very good Korean, and I speak Mandarin, Shandong, Shanghai, English, Cantonese, Japanese. I spoke French when I was young, but now I've forgotten most of it. Because I stayed in Korea for two years and had a Korean girlfriend, I learned to speak Korean. I stayed in Bangkok for two years and learned to speak very good Thai at that time. And I speak Taiwanese and Mandarin.

Taiwanese is a totally different language. Most of my languages come as a result of where I'm filming. When I stayed in Spain for six months, I spoke very good Spanish: "*Como está?*" Every morning, when I was filming with all the film crews.

That's got to make you even more popular globally, because you are not just restricted to the language of the region that you happened to be born into. I can't think of any other actor who has that capacity to speak so many languages. That's a huge accomplishment. It really is.

[smiles] Yeah, well.

Why is it that you travel so much to make your films?

Hollywood or American actors and directors are very lucky. Why? You have a very big country. Also, you have the technology. Whenever you want to go and have a stunt done, the actor's or actress's life is so valuable that they don't have to do it; instead you can turn it into a special-effect thing. Then, they think about the blue background. You work on it, draw the airplane to do the computer graphic. You make the actor's job so much easier this way. And the actor is so busy that they don't want to go to, say, Germany or Paris to film a scene. OK, you send the photographers over there to film some exteriors and then come back and when the movie comes out, it looks as though you're sitting in Paris. No, everything was shot in an L.A. studio. For us, our lives are so cheap, we have to do our own stunts. Everybody has to do their own stunts. We can't afford the blue background, so we have to go to Paris. The whole crew has to move to Paris to shoot the whole thing. So all those years I've been moving around, and moving around, so much so that—especially in Hong Kong right now—people call me "Ghengis Kong" and the people who are with me are the "Mongolians." Every place I stay not more than one year. Last year I stayed four months in South Africa, three months in Rotterdam, one to two weeks in Taiwan, two weeks in Japan, one month in Malaysia, five days in Hong Kong, and then I came to the United States for two weeks; then I went back to Malaysia and now I'm back in the United States. And then next year, it will be Paris and Turkey. All those years—Yugoslavia, South America, North America—I've been everywhere with all the crew.

It would seem that you would learn new things—receive an "education," in other words, from each of your travels, which is something that most actors—scratch that, most people—would never get.

Yeah, I believe so. Right now, when you see my movies there are many things going on. For example, when you see *Armor of God II: Operation Condor*, with all the wind tunnel things, the film starts out about the pursuit of gold, but in the end the most valuable thing is water. "I don't want gold, I want water!" Why? Because when I got there I found out that, really, the water is very expensive. There was a girl who had to walk, like, six hours to get two bucketfuls of water for her home. All her life, her whole life, is taking care of the water needs for her family. She gets up at four o'clock in the morning—walk, walk, walk, walk—three hours to get some water. And then—walk, walk, walk, walk—coming back. Then she puts the water in a big tank. Then—walk, walk, walk, walk—back to get some more water. She kept going right through the night! She did this for her family to take care of their needs for food, for taking a shower. Even just to have a short

The great man at the Great Wall. For a video documentary made on his life entitled *The Jackie Chan Story*, Jackie and his crew went on location to the Great Wall of China.

shower would require her to walk for hours to get enough water. The next morning she would be back at it again—walk, walk, walk, walk—for her whole life! When she gets married, has a son or a daughter, then the daughter would take over. That's when I found out that the water is so much more important than gold. The city people open the water taps and leave them open when they brush their teeth, wash their hands, take a bath, have a shower—but when I learned about what this girl went through to bring water to my hotel, I turned mine off. Because I was in there, I saw how important the water was—and what she had to go through.

When I was filming in another location, I found out that the local people were killing each other. Why? Because of religion. So, in *Armor of God*, I'm talking about religion. And when I was filming *Who Am I?* in Africa, I found out that people were killing animals and destroying the environment. Then, in the movie, besides my entertainment, I wanted to put in a little bit of a message. So now, in *Miracles*,

I'm talking about the Mafia. I'm talking about the triads. I don't mind. In the movie I also play a triad and I have my character tell the triads, "What are you going to do when you get old? When your grandchildren ask you, 'Grandfather, what did you do?' are you going to say, 'I was a kidnapper'— are you going to say those kinds of things? You should be ashamed!" I say that in my movie, because I know that a lot of triads will come and see my movie. That's the education. I'm telling them, "Now you're young, when you're sixteen years old you can get money this way, by kidnapping somebody or robbing somebody, but what about when you are sixty or eighty years old? When your children ask you, 'Father, or Grandfather, when you were sixteen, when you were young, what did you do?' Will you say these kinds of things to your children?" I don't know if they will listen or not, but at least I will have done my job to present on the screen, to the audience, what is right.

You seem to bring a lot of social consciousness to your films.

I always tell the actors and actresses in Hong Kong, "We have a responsibility to do something positive for society. We should show bad things on the screen as little as possible, because we are the role models. Everybody watches us. Everybody wants to copy us as role models. If, for example, you have the hero in a movie take a cigarette out of his mouth and throw it on the floor, everybody will then take their cigarettes out and think that it's all right to throw them on the floor. That's a bad thing. How many children have learned from movies that it's OK to kill people? Too many. They rob banks, rape women, these kinds of things. So in my movie, even if somebody else drops a newspaper, I will have my character go and pick it up and throw it in the wastepaper basket. Why? Maybe you don't care, but I care. I don't care if you care or not, but I, myself, do care. That's my responsibility.

Traveling the world like you have, spending time getting to know people and observing their cultures, you've become a citizen of the world and not just of Hong Kong or America. Do you find that every culture then embraces you as one of their own?

Yes, I believe so.

"I'm not a superstar. That's just my job. I have to promote peace. I have to do the best that I can for the real human being concerns."—Jackie Chan

Because the truths that you teach in your films go beyond race, they go beyond countries.

Yes, it seems especially so with me. I don't know why. No matter where I go, ever since I started in films—of course, I'm more popular now than when I started; more people know me now, especially in countries like South Africa. We were in the middle of nowhere and these natives came up to me and started chanting, "Jackie Chan! Jackie Chan!" They only had one video of mine! Right now, they are still watching *Drunken Master*—still! They just know all the moves I did in that movie, like the snake hand techniques, and it just, well, it really surprised me. Even in Morocco, in the Sahara, people know me. And they treat me like a king. But I just tell myself, "No, I'm not a superstar. That's just my job. I have to promote peace. I have to do the best that I can for the real human being concerns." I don't know. I guess because I didn't "suddenly" become a big star. I was a child actor, then a low-class stuntman, then I became a stunt coordinator, an actor. All those things.

Given where you've come from, do you find it amazing that you have as much influence as you do? I mean, you actually affect people's lives, which is pretty amazing when you think about it. I mean, you're not just making movies, you're affecting people's lives with what you do. Even something as mundane as picking up the garbage in one of your movies, some kid is going to see that and think, "Hey, if Jackie Chan can pick up garbage, then it's cool for me to do it, too."

Jackie is keenly aware that whenver he goes out in public, whether at a charity benefit or simply walking the streets of Hong Kong, Sydney, or Beverly Hills's famous Rodeo Drive, his actions can serve to affect people's lives. It's a responsibility that he takes very seriously.

Yes, even them. [gestures towards his stuntmen] I teach them now that when they go out for a walk, they should pick up the rubbish from the ground. I'm so happy. At least my company, the J. C. Group, even they pick up garbage. Because if everybody would pick up one piece of rubbish from the floor, then the whole of L.A. would become very clean.

It must be a very good feeling for you to know that you can so positively affect people in such a manner.

Well, really I should thank you. I should thank the audience for supporting me. Because of them, my career has changed. I wasn't born to become a

good person, I'm not a god. No. I was a bad child. A long time ago I went around fighting on the street. I wanted to fight, I wanted to see how powerful I could be, how powerful my punch was, how fast my kick was, and how fast I could run. And then later on I found out that this was wrong. That was wrong. Then, later on, after I started making movies, I found out how much the audience supported me and it struck me, "Wow, so many children go to see my movies."

When I first became famous, I didn't want anything to do with charities. People would come up to me and say, "Jackie Chan, would you please help out our charity?" And I'd say, "No, I'm too busy. I want to go to a disco, I want to have fun." Then on one occasion a person came up and asked me to go to a charity. They said, "Would you please go—just for one day? Just say 'hello'? The children really *need* to see you." I said, "No, I'm busy." But then, for whatever reason, I changed my mind and said, "OK, I'll go—but make it quick. I'll give you fifteen minutes." Then when we got to the children's hospital I saw these children with no legs, some couldn't speak, they were sick but they were so happy to see me! My being there actually made a difference in their lives! Then the people announced, "Jackie Chan has bought a lot of presents for you children, and now he would like to present them to you." I hadn't bought them any presents! But they had already prepared all these presents to make the kids happy. I asked the people, "What's this?" They said, "I don't know." I was mad. I said, "You don't know? But you're the ones who bought them!" They just said, "Would you please just give them out to the children?" So I started to give them out, one by one, to the children. They were so happy, some were crying. I touched them, they cried. I shook their hands and they would tell me, "I'll never wash my hand again!"

It made me upset inside to think, "Who the heck am I? Who?" I suddenly looked at myself in the mirror. Why did I have so much power to help these children? Then to find out that I was cheating those children— the presents weren't purchased by me! Somebody bought them for me. The children asked me as I was leaving, "Are you coming back to us next year?" I

Jackie's exposure to underprivileged children in Hong Kong opened his eyes to the importance of helping out his fellow man. Ever since, Jackie has been a tireless supporter of children's and senior citizens' charities all around the world. He even encourages all of his co-stars to do likewise, saying, "Once you're involved—you're involved! I like to have everybody involved because if everybody helped everybody, how pretty is the world?"

knew what I had to do. "Yes, I'm coming back," I said. Then I turned around and told the people who had asked me to attend, "I'm coming back next year. Let me know what time, what day—and I'll buy *my own* presents." Then that next year, I went to buy a whole bunch of trucks and toys and went back to see those children again. I was so happy because I wasn't there under false pretenses. This time it was true. "Here, here, here." [gestures giving out gifts] And when the children asked me, "Are you coming back again next year, Jackie?" I said, "Yes!"

Then another children's school requested my appearance, and I said "Yes" to that, too. And I promised to go back to that one again. And this just grew from Hong Kong to Las Vegas. Why would I go to Las Vegas like I did this year to do a free show? Because I know that the proceeds are going to go to help charity. Last year I did a benefit for the elderly in San Francisco—and I'll be going back again this year. Then I did the charity at the MGM Grand Hotel. Over 14,000 people came to see me and I gave all the money, over $200,000, to the elderly. I wasn't doing it for the public posture it gives me but doing it naturally. And everybody I work with, the actors, the actresses, I tell them, "Go! Do it!" They are like me, hesitant at first, but once you're involved—you're involved! I like to have everybody involved because if everybody helped everybody, how pretty is the world? Now it seems that everybody is just interested in taking care of themselves. I mean, don't get me wrong, I take care of myself, too. That's OK. We should. But everybody should look after everybody. That's my philosophy. Of course, I know that it's difficult. It's hard. But I just try to do the best I can. Maybe one day you'll try the best you can. If everybody just tells everybody, then ten people will tell ten people. It grows. And maybe not this generation, and maybe not the second generation—but by the third generation, everybody is becoming good.

What are your thoughts on the current political situation in Hong Kong, what with the Chinese takeover from Great Britain?

Of course, I'm Chinese. I hope China becomes big. Like in America, they say, "I'm proud to be an American." One day, I hope there will be that same sense of pride when a Chinese person says, "I'm proud to be Chinese." Why is it that every Chinese immigrates to some other country? Why are American people not immigrating to China? Why is everybody going away? That shows we are ashamed. Why were we Chinese scared when China took back

Hong Kong? You'd think that we should be happy. But then everybody was scared. "We don't like China," they'd say. Why? Everybody immigrated to Canada and America—why? Maybe I'm too idealistic. I realize that there are no perfect things, but I would like things to be perfect. I want everybody to be, like, "We're Chinese, we have a good government." I know it's difficult. Everybody in China and Hong Kong was going on about the government. I said, "Do something for the Chinese government. Do something for your government. Don't always tell the government, 'Do something for me!' You sit there, you throw the rubbish on the floor, you throw your cigarettes on the floor, you're the ones who have screwed up everything—you're not helping your country." You just sit there and say, "We need this and this." No. If you don't have the strength to help your government, then help yourself. Help your country—pick up something, at least. Yeah, that's my philosophy.

If I cannot help my government do something, then at least I can do my best to make my movies the best that I can. Then people say, "Ah, Jackie's from Hong Kong." I let people know I'm from Hong Kong. I pick up some rubbish if I'm in my own country. I do some smiling for the tourists. If I can help the tourists, then more tourists will come to Hong Kong to help our businesses. That's what I'm doing. I'm not sitting around blaming the government. The government has a lot of things to do. That's what I'm thinking. Because all those years, no matter where—the U.S., the Philippines, China—everywhere, people just complained, "We don't like George Bush!" Now, it's "We don't like President Clinton!" Well, now we've changed the whole Chinese government, and even if we changed to some other person, the people would say, "We don't like you!" It's a never-ending story. Always going on and on. None of the presidents were perfect. Even Lincoln, somebody shot him, right? None of our presidents stay there, in a position where they can say, "I'm the best!" And all the people go, "Yeah!" I'm not a political person—I do my own job and try to help my country that way.

Is there a lot of dissent from Chinese people outside of Hong Kong who are complaining about the new government?

Well, at that time a lot of Chinese immigrated to Canada, and then it was when coming back to Hong Kong that they said, "Oh, we don't like the Chinese government!" To them I say, "Shut up! You're not *Chinese* anymore. You're *Canadian*. Go away." I say, "Go away!"

Really?

Yeah! I tell them, "You suppose you're Chinese after you immigrate to Canada? You have a Canadian passport and now you're coming back saying, 'Down with China! We don't like China!' You're making a problem for those of us who stayed! You went away. Let our Chinese resolve our problems. You're not Chinese anymore. You're Canadian." That's what I'm saying. I hate those kinds of people. I'll tell you why I don't like those kinds of people; all right, some people for some reason immigrate—OK—because generation after generation go. That doesn't matter. But these other people, they move to China and from China they skip to Hong Kong. They stay in Hong Kong for seven years. After seven years they get a passport. Then they find out China will be taking back Hong Kong, so they move to Canada. After the Canadian government says that they don't want any more Chinese, or if they encounter racial problems in Canada, these people get scared, so they move to America. They get scared again when they experience an earthquake in L.A., so they move to Singapore. Those kinds of people are useless. They never help the country they are in—they just want to find a good country. Now, because Singapore's laws are so strict—they are holding a Singapore passport now—so they go back to Hong Kong. I hate those kinds of people.

Do you see a lot of that in Hong Kong these days?

Yes! Yes! I stay in Hong Kong because I have to give the people confidence. And I help my country so that it can become the best country.

You could have gone to, say, America and said, "Oh, the Communists are coming to Hong Kong, I'm going to take my money and go to America." But you didn't do that.

No. I had to let six million people see that I'm staying. I trust our government. Everybody was saying, "Let's give the policemen trouble. Let's give the government trouble." I say, leave the government alone to make our roads better, to improve our airport, and things like that. The citizens should do their part to pick up the rubbish and help to keep the city clean. Let's try and make Hong Kong the cleanest city in the world. That's what I would do. That's what I would promote. I don't know—maybe a lot of people, after they read this will say, "Screw you, Jackie! You're full of crap!" OK, that's my thinking. You asked me, so I'm telling you my thoughts on the matter. Maybe I'm wrong. Maybe I'm wrong and too idealistic. No matter

Whether in real life or in the movies, Jackie always makes sure that the decency of his character is his top priority.

what anybody else says, I'll do my own thing. I'm happy. You don't want to pick up the rubbish, OK. I'll pick up the rubbish and make myself happy.

How would you like to be remembered when people look back on you 100 years from now?

I want the people to remember that I was a person like Buster Keaton or John Wayne or Harold Lloyd. Remember me. That's all. One day I want my children and grandchildren to say, "Yes, that's my grandfather." I don't want to do something that would bring shame to my family—I don't want to make terrible pictures, so that when people talk about me they say, "Ah, he was awful." That's no good. I want them to think of my work and say, "Ah, *Drunken Master II*!" "Oh, did you see *Police Story*?" "Oh, yes!" "Wasn't it good?" "Ah, it was great!"

A thoughtful man, Jackie says, "I don't want to do something that would bring shame to my family—I don't want to make terrible pictures."

On Success

For years the Hong Kong entertainment industry has referred to Jackie as "Dai Goh," or "big brother," because of the prosperity he has continued to bring year after year to the Hong Kong film industry and the number of jobs his films and various entrepreneurial enterprises have created.

"From his first leading man role through January 1995," says *Variety*'s Derek Elley, "pictures starring Jackie Chan have grossed the equivalent of eighty million in U.S. dollars at the Hong Kong box office," seventy million of those dollars since Chan signed with Golden Harvest for the 1980 release *Young Master*. These figures do not include "hunky revenues" from Japan, Taiwan, South Korea, Malaysia, Singapore, and Thailand. "It is said that none of the forty-plus Hong Kong movies Chan has starred in has incurred a loss," wrote *Hollywood Reporter* reviewer Whang Yeeling. It seems that everything the young superstar touches turns to pure platinum.

Jackie, a lot of people in this country obviously look at you as being the ultimate in successful. What do you think are the secrets to your success?

I think there's a lot of audiences who know me and know that my road to success has not been overnight but rather a process extending some thirty-five years. Some other new audiences think, "Wow, Jackie Chan is a big star!" They think I've become a big star overnight. No, I've been through a lot of painful ups and downs. I don't know and I don't care what image I have or how the audiences see me. I know who I am. I always have my feet on the ground. You treat me, say, as a big star, then I become a big star. But I never treat myself as a big star. I just treat myself as a fellow with a job and that job is to make better movies. Besides making a movie, besides making money, I have a responsibility. That's all. Then making movies is my choice. I have fun. Everyday I have fun with the 300 or 400 people who are on the set with me. I'm like the leader who can control everybody. And that's the most fun part. My films are like toys and it's as if I can make fun toys to show, like, a billion people. That's the most fun thing about it. If you are talking about success, there are far more people who are far more successful than me. My dream was simply to have everybody in the whole world know me, like the dinosaurs or like E.T.

"My films are like toys and it's as if I can make fun toys to show, like, a billion people."—Jackie Chan

You've certainly achieved that. Is there anything you've found in your career that has helped you to become successful—obviously, you said you've been through over thirty-five years of ups and downs—but what is it that has helped you keep going on this roller-coaster ride?

I think the audience. And also I always play a game with myself to find an enemy for myself. It's this kind of game that makes things interesting for me. Every movie I have a different character to play and that the company pays me a lot of money to get me to play. Of course, my films do not have as big a budget as American movies, but in my country, in Asia, I have the biggest production budget. They give me thirty million, thirty-five or forty million. Then I can play all the games, like: I want to hire you, but I don't want to hire you, I want this, I want that. Then I can play.

What are the ingredients or qualities that go into making you so successful?

Well, the audience. First, of course, I want money—for living. After I get the money, I find out that for a film to be successful a lot of people have to go to see it. Then I get the support from the audience and not just the Asian audience. There was the Indian, Malaysian, Vietnam, Thai, Korean—everybody. They send me flowers for Valentine's Day, for Christmas. Then I find out a lot of parents write to me: "My son thinks you're a role model. Please write to him and encourage him to do well in school." Then I find out I have a responsibility, so I have to make better movies. Either then I make twenty movies a year or I make one movie a year. But I know that I could guarantee myself that that one movie I could make *really* good. How could I make twenty movies, all with dangerous stunts? I might die soon if I did that. OK,

Jackie (left) and one of his top stuntmen, Mars (right), in the 1982 sequel to *Young Master, Dragon Lord.*

I want to make good movies. Aside from making money, I want to make good movies.

Then later on I find an enemy in Asia; this company or actor is almost as good as me, so I want to knock him down. I want to make a better and better movie so that I can beat this action star. At the time there were several action stars in Asia, but I don't want a few, I want one—me. Because this other fellow would make five or six movies in a year, the audience was seeing him every three months and were starting to get tired of him. Then Jackie Chan's movie comes out, with the best things in it, and it's always different than any other movie. When you make five movies, I have a chance to watch you in four movies, then I know what direction you're heading in, which tells me that I should be doing something completely different. That way, my movies are always fresh.

Pretty soon nobody in Asia can compete with me. The Asian scene was no longer giving me any challenges to overcome, so then I started looking at the American movies. So then I have to find a new "enemy" to beat in the American movies. Let's say I choose Sylvester Stallone. OK, I like Stallone, but let's say that he has become my new target. I find out different things—if

Jackie has always wanted to be popular in America in addition to Southeast Asia. His first American-made film, *The Big Brawl*, did not become the success he had hoped for. Only after Jackie was allowed to be himself and present his own unique personality on the screen did American audiences begin to embrace him.

he uses special effects I'm not going to use them. American directors think they can make anybody into an action star, but when the people watch their action movies they think only of Jackie Chan. So after awhile I became very popular in America where they consider my movies and stunt coordinating very outstanding. I know I've paid the price for this position—broken fingers, broken ankle, this kind of thing.[6] But I like it. I want to be different than the others. I don't want to be Superman, and I don't want to be Batman, because you or anybody can be Batman or Superman—but nobody, or at least very few people, can be Jackie Chan. Then when I found this out I thought, "Good, I want to be a Jackie Chan." So only making one movie a year, I have a lot of time for researching what kind of locations, action, and comedy I want to put in my film. I'm always making notes on these things—"I want this for my next movie," "I want this for another movie," "This one for *Police Story*," "This one for *Police Story V*," and so on. I always write it down. So this way I think the audience is the most important ingredient in pushing me on. I'm like a train, and the audience and fans are what keep me going down the track.

Do you ever find it strange that despite being Jackie Chan, and the position you enjoy within the film industry, you can't always make the films you want to?

The whole film industry is very strange! [laughing] I know some of the problems, for my "Eastern Western," the script isn't finalized. And if we make this film, we will have to film it in the U.S. and deal with so many unions and things. I will be using a lot of Americans for cast and crew. They won't work like a Hong Kong crew and take just ten minutes for lunch—they have set times for everything and I can't afford to be like in Hong Kong and spend three months doing the ending. Even when we filmed in Canada the crew was very good, but as soon as it's time for lunch, everybody stops! In Hong Kong the crew will sometimes work and eat at the same time. For this movie I have to make a very good plan and schedule or else I will be in a lot of trouble when we are filming. (JC/PNP)

Some big Hollywood celebrities get their "star" on the Walk of Fame. But only the most internationally famous are treated to a cement-print ceremony at Mann's Chinese Theatre. One of Jackie's biggest wishes came true on Sunday, January 5, 1997, when he was asked to place his hands, shoes —and nose!—in cement in front of the famous Hollywood movie theater.

You're very much a role model and public figure— a spokesman for AIDS Concern, the Royal Hong Kong Police Force uses your Police Story theme tune in its recruitment ads, you're the tourist ambassador for Hong Kong. Do you find that because of your position in the public eye, you have to be a bit more responsible?

You know that I don't ask for any of these things. People observe the way I behave and then ask me to assume these duties. I'm like a goodwill ambassador. The police call me up and ask me to give some awards, so I do it. AIDS Concern asks me to help, so I try my best to help. I feel very proud when people refer to me as a role model or think highly of me, so I try harder to be responsible and not let people down. (JC/PNP)

You always seem to be working, Jackie, either in front of the camera or behind it as a producer. Doing charity work, singing, launching new business ventures such as the *"Star Shops" and your soft drink "Bobo Cha,"* or giving up your time for interviews. How do you relax?

Relax! I don't have any free time, how can I relax? My schedule is always full, my secretaries arrange everything for me and then they give me a timetable. Today you are interviewing me, then tomorrow I will fly to Taiwan for two days, then go to Malaysia; then I am presenting some dialysis machines to a hospital, then it's off to Singapore, then China, and then to Japan for location hunting. I'm very busy! I need a holiday! (JC/PNP)

You're also quite a singer, aren't you?

I sing a lot, but I'm not a professional singer. However, I do sing very well.

Are you going to be doing any albums?

"In all my movies I always say good things about the police and I have a very good relationship with the police officers." Jackie upholding the law—this time as a lawyer—in 1987's *Dragons Forever.*

No, because the way I do an album is almost like the way I do a film. The last album I did took me three years to finish! So I would rather spend three years and make one movie!

Given that you are now very famous and that you represent a lot of money to a lot of people, which, as we touched upon earlier, is something that the triads are very interested in, how do you deal with the triads today?

You mean now?

Yes.

No, they stay away from me. They stay away from you when you get too big.

Really? I would have thought that it would have been just the opposite.

No, because all these years I've been doing a lot of things for charity. I'm the image in Asia that is against the triads. I'm the model of the police. In all my movies I always say good things about the police and I have a very good relationship with the police officers. And also the triads know that if I have a problem, then they have a problem too. I'm the one who stands up and says to the newspapers, "Come on, triads. Come to my office and destroy it—come on!" I'm staying right here and will lead the people marching against the triads. With the triads, if you take one step back, they'll take one step forward. Then, if you go forward, they move backward. The triads are always in the darkness—when you take out a flashlight and shine it on them, they scurry away and hide. You have to fight back. Most of the time I concentrate on . . . let me put it this way—if I'm doing something bad, of course it would be very easy for the triads to get to me because I would need their help. But I'm always on the good side. If I say something like, "You are wrong! You are wrong—why are you threatening this girl? Go away!" They say, "OK," and go away. That's the way to be.

Obviously you are the first one that we've heard about who has done that. Were you a little nervous when you first decided to stand up to the triads?

Ummm, yeah—but someone had to do it. And after you do it, you find out, yeah, everybody backs me up on this, and you find out that you have a lot of support, and that gives you much more confidence. Then you just keep speaking out again, and again, and again to protect some other witnesses.

You mentioned earlier that you dared them to come and disrupt your office. Had they threatened to do this to you?

No, I just said it to them. I said, "I'm here in my office right now. Come here and destroy it—if you have the guts. Come!" Nobody came. If you don't say it, that's when they will come.

Jackie fielded questions and signed autographs for his many fans during a two-hour stint at the Los Angeles Comic Book and Science Fiction Convention.

What was the reaction of the people of Hong Kong when you did that?

Everybody applauded me. I got a lot of phone calls the next morning, with people saying, "I saw what you did in the newspapers! That's good! It's about time we found somebody to stand up to them and say those things!"

You led a march against the triads in Hong Kong, didn't you?

Yes. Also, I think I'm quite different from most actors in Hong Kong in that I'm always moving around. When I come into Hong Kong and people come up to me and say, "Jackie, we need your help, would you say something on our behalf?" I say, "OK," and do what needs to be done. But then I get with my group and we'll fly off to Malaysia to film for six months, and then come back to Hong Kong and do something else. I don't just stay in Hong Kong these days, I'm traveling around all over the world. But, still, everybody knows I'm from Hong Kong, and I try to help Hong Kong in many ways. I help the Hong Kong film industry and try to always do good things. Then, after that, I go off to make my own movies. After I spoke out against the triads, everybody in Hong Kong just calls me "Big Brother."

On Films and Filmmaking

More than a phenomenon, Jackie Chan is a one-man industry. Jackie Chan fan clubs all over the world send emissaries to the sets of his films, which he often writes, directs, and produces, using equipment rented from companies he has created to improve the technical quality of Hong Kong filmmaking. He was instrumental in forming a stunt professionals union, and hiring men and women who belong to the Jackie Chan Stuntmen's Association. In addition, he hires actors supplied by his own casting and model agency, "Jackie's Angels."

Jackie Chan embodies the cheerful entrepreneurial energy that has made Hong Kong the only national cinema that can compete on its home turf with Hollywood. But all that energy is expended toward improving his art, for Jackie Chan is the kind of filmmaker who lives and breathes film. "Once you are making movies," he once told fans in Chicago, "it's like a drug—you can't not do it."

How did you first get involved in filmmaking?

When I was eight, a production company contacted my master about providing them with child actors. The female lead in my first movie was the hottest star in Hong Kong and Taiwan at that time. Over her next several movies she picked me to play her son. So my name as a child actor got built up in the industry. Then when I entered the period where you are no longer

Jackie always comes up with new ideas for his action sequences. One of his most imaginative film battles took place in an underwater shark tank in the film *First Strike* (a.k.a. *Police Story IV*). Courtesy of Nova Friedman.

a child, but not yet a man, I had trouble finding parts. But as I grew bigger, they hired me on as a stuntman. From that I became an assistant martial arts choreographer, and later, the official choreographer. My specific job was to teach people how to react to punches for the camera. The directors and producers decided that I reacted to punches, and acted the parts, much better than some of their male leads. They wanted me to be an actor as well as a technical coordinator. And that's how it all began. (IJC)

Is there a difference in the type of people who go to see your films and the ones who go to see those made by other action stars in Hong Kong?

One of my movies has been released right now in Asia and I just got the press reviews from Hong Kong. When people go to the theater to see my film, they are not surrounded by the young kids in the yellow hats with the earrings through their noses. These kids go to see the triad-produced films—they want to see the triad movies. But everybody can bring their children to a Jackie Chan movie. Everybody feels comfortable bringing their

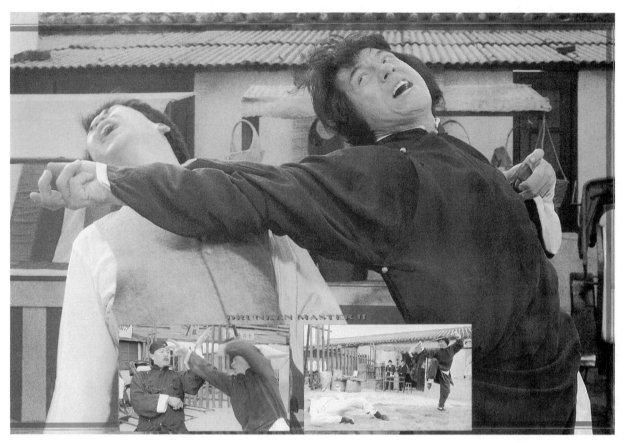

One of Jackie's greatest kung-fu battles took place in *Drunken Master II*. He considers it one of the best fight scenes he's ever filmed.

children to a Jackie Chan movie. When I'm fighting on screen, all the children are smiling and laughing. The children are smiling and the big people are excited, saying, "Oh, yeah! Look at that!" That's my audience, and that's the only audience I want.

You released **Drunken Master II** *to great success both domestically and internationally. The film was the sequel to the classic* **Drunken Master,** *the film that first brought you success. A lot of people were implying that the film was out of control and would fail at the box office. However, the film was a huge success with audiences and critics worldwide. Looking back at the film, are you happy with it?*

Not really. Of course I am happy that it was very successful in Asia and internationally, but, to tell the truth, I am not 100 percent satisfied with the film. If from the very beginning I had been the director myself, it would have been a better film and very different in style from the released one. If I am just an actor in a film, then I have time to do other things, so I invited Lau Chia Liang to direct. He was a very good director,[7] and when I spoke to him I could see that he wanted to make a good film too. But I don't think his directing style is up to date; the film looks like an old movie. I wasn't always in China during the early part of filming, I was very busy on some other projects, so a lot of the film was already in the can without me seeing it. I had very high expectations of Lau Chia Liang, so later when I saw the footage I was disappointed and thought the film would not do too well at the box office and the audiences would be very disappointed. But I respect Lau Chia Liang so I did not say anything and we continued filming. We were making the film for the Hong Kong Stuntman's Association (HKSA), but when the members of the HKSA board of directors saw the film, they were shocked and said there is no way they could release the film as it was. I suggested that maybe if they let me redirect some scenes and film some new ones, then we could salvage the film. So the HKSA board sat down with Lau Chia Liang and told him that they were not satisfied with the film—but it's not like they were firing him. . . . (JC/PNP)

It's strange, because certain elements of the Hong Kong press and some Western magazines/writers tried to accuse you of firing him, pushing him off the film.

No, it was the decision of the HKSA, not me. They asked me to take over. And to speak the truth, when the movie comes out and it's not a success, who would people first say is the reason for its failure? First is me, then Golden Harvest who releases the film, thirdly the HKSA, and then, finally, Lau Chia Liang. So they spoke to Lau Chia Liang, and I set to work reshooting and reworking the film. Lau Chia Liang had shot over 9,000 feet of film by the time he finished. I cut 4,000 feet and reshot, redubbed, reworked, and reedited for the next few months. I know that Lau Chia Liang is not happy with the HKSA decision, but it's not my fault. Then he announced that he was going to make *Drunken Master III*, his way—"To show people the real Joy Kun/Drunken Boxing." That makes me feel strange. *Drunken Master II* still says Lau Chia Liang is the director, and when it's released it's a great success and everyone has a very high opinion of him. Then he goes and makes *Drunken Master III*, and what happened? It failed at the box office, the audience didn't like it, and everyone changed their opinion of Lau Chia Liang. (JC/PNP)

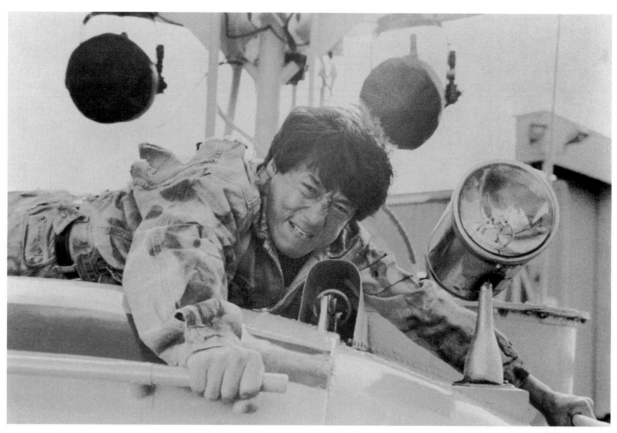

Rumble in the Bronx is the film that catapulted Jackie to superstardom in North America.

When you were first starting out and becoming famous, I remember you saying that "Bruce Lee did it his way, so I'm going to do it the opposite way"—like yin and yang—but you always did your own unique thing.

Well, I always wanted to do something that was different from all the other movies. That's what makes what I do special. Look right now at the American movies—and everything right now is a big explosion. "My explosion is going to be bigger than your explosion," type of thing. When I did explosions, that was ten years ago! *Police Story II* dealt with everything you could think of about explosions. The whole movie, you can find out, the explosions were hitting my body, in my eyes, in my head, then from the small explosions to, at the end, the big explosion. Then, after that, I stopped doing it. In *Police Story*, I did everything with breaking glass—glass, glass, glass—the whole movie was breaking glass things. Then, with *Miracles*, I played with some other things. Then I found out that in America, during these same two years, everything was explosions. Then I tell myself, "My movie is not going to use any more big explosions." Small explosions and

Jackie said of *Rumble in the Bronx*: "After I did *The Big Brawl* (1980), I stayed behind in America to study English, and I got the idea for doing a story where I'd come to America as a student and tangle with a local gang. I had to change it a little from my original concept, so I made my character a Hong Kong cop on vacation."

more difficult action scenes. So that's what made me and my movies different from Hollywood movies. I'm always watching some other movie and then doing something different as a result of having seen it. That's what makes mine special.

One thing that seems apparent to me is that as you've become more and more successful and have gained more and more control over your films, more and more of your philosophy and beliefs have found their way into your films. How do you decide on what to include in your films?

I don't know, I just shoot whatever I like to shoot. I don't care about the market so much. Right now you can see—especially in Asia—the gangster or triad movies are very successful, so now everyone is making triad movies. No matter how big the star is, every big star now makes triad movies. And if some kung-fu movie becomes a success, then everybody will go in the direction of making more kung-fu movies. Me? I always turn it around. When they're making a kung-fu movie, I'm making *Police Story*. When they make *Police Story*–type films, then I'll go back to making a kung-fu movie. It seems that I have to prove the success of a particular type of film, and then they follow my lead. When they were making movies like the Wong Fei Hung[8] series, which was a great success, I decided that I'm not going to make that type of movie. When everybody stops making this sort of movie, that's when I'll make it. They always ask me, "Why? Why are you now making this type of movie when it's already lost its popularity?" I say, "No." I have to prove to them that the audience is bright, and that they will always choose to go to a good movie.

Even now in Asia the movie business market is very bad, and all the film people just say, "Oh yes, the market is very bad because the audience now wants to save money, so they're staying home. Now what can we do?" I say, "No—look at *Titanic*. Everywhere it's breaking records. Why? Because if it's a good movie, people will always go to see it." Now, my movie, *Who Am I?* has been released in Asia, and everybody's going to see it. Why? Because the audience is not as dumb as the market watchers think. If it's a good movie, the people will always go to see it. No matter how low the business side or market gets, the good things people will always buy. The good movie they will always go to see. Similarly, the worst music, nobody listens to it. Good music everybody listens to. So that fact I trust.

1984's *Wheels on Meals* was to be a modern-day *Three Musketeers*, complete with sword fighting and a damsel in distress. It also reunited "the three Musketeers" of Hong Kong cinema, Jackie Chan (left), Sammo Hung (center), and Yuen Biao (right).

So you don't tend to be influenced by the vicissitudes of the market in regard to your moviemaking plans.

After all these years in the film business, I never look at it as "up and down." It is always "up." Even in Malaysia right now, I'm the only one who has a film that has outgrossed *Titanic*. [laughs] Of course, in most countries, *Titanic* is the biggest hit—but at least in one country I have beaten *Titanic*. And that makes me happy. It doesn't matter, of course, if I lose out to *Titanic*, it's a 200-million-dollar film! What's my cost? I'm running around nineteen million and something, so it should do nineteen times more than what my picture does. But if I win—ha, ha, ha! If I can beat James Bond, 007, I feel the same way. They are American productions with big budgets—hundreds of millions of dollars per film—if I lose to them, that's OK. But if I win, it's even more of an accomplishment. I'm so proud of myself that with my kind of budget I can beat those big-budget films.

You mentioned that you read a lot. What kind of books do you like?

I like a lot of science books and science fiction. I read a lot of *National Geographic*, also. They bring me to really different locations and make me

One of *Operation Condor's* most entertaining sequences featured Jackie's fight against Ken Lo in a wind tunnel.

want to film in these places. I also like *Reader's Digest* and read a lot of movie books.

To many people, you've become so much more than an action actor, they consider you a teacher—but on a big, global scale. Why did this happen?

Because I learned so many things. The Chinese have a saying that goes, *It is better to travel one thousand miles than to go to school for one year.* Why when I make a movie is it better than other people's? Because when they make their movie, they do it out of a school book: *dolly, zoom.* And if they don't have a dolly, they don't know how to make the movie. I'm different. I was growing up in a very poor movie business. We never had a dolly in Chinese films. I had to make my own dolly out of a wheelchair, or a bicycle. We just took things that were flexible. We didn't have a crane, so what did we do? We took a ladder and took the screws off and used man-power—four people—to lift the ladder with the camera on it. That became our crane. So we make movies easy. But when I look at the American technology I'm impressed—the crane design here, the Steadicam design there, the dolly—wow! But without those, they don't know how to make movies! They use a computer, they use a tablecam, a flyingcam. I never heard about those kinds of things! What we are using is a "peoplecam." We are helping the cameraman by pulling on a wire to help raise him up for the shot: "One, two, three—here we go!" But Americans never use the wire hooking a camera up to two stories, and then lowering it down. But we do that because we don't have their kind of technology. What I learn I teach people. What I say to you today, I learned from somebody else. I learn good things from somebody and then I teach somebody who doesn't know these things.

"Why, when I make this movie, does it make me nervous and make me want to tell the director how to do it? Well, the reason is that I care about my movies."
—Jackie Chan

Your interest in making a film—unlike a lot of actors who say "I want to make sure my name is above the credits," or "I have to be paid so much to act in this film," and that's all they care about—is a very deep and personal

thing. You see yourself as having a real responsibility and you feel a certain passion for what you do. Is this an accurate assessment?

Yes. When I do see some other American actors, I want less money. "Please let me get this job." Like when Marlon Brando auditioned for *The Godfather,* he made himself up and really went all out for that part—that is a true *professional.* Why did Madonna write a ten-page letter to the director of *Evita,* telling him why she wanted that role? I respect this kind of actor. Some others just say, "I want ten million," "I want fifteen million," "I want twenty million." If I simply wanted money, I could make ten movies in any one year. Why every year do I just make one movie? Why do I let other people direct me, when I have directed very successfully in the past? I can sit here, like I am now, and be truly nervous about the film I am in. Why, when I make this movie, does it make me nervous and make me want to tell the director how to do it? Well, the reason is that I care about my movies. It is like my son with his toys. Even now, my writer is coming to my trailer and we will prepare the script for my next movie. Making movies is fun. I can make something, and then after I've completed it I can enjoy watching people enjoy what I've made. That's what I want. It's like my own video

"I've done so many things, sometimes even I forget what I've done. And when I finally get a chance to look at these films, I go 'Wow! I really did do a lot of good things.'"—Jackie Chan

Armor of God, shot on location in Yugoslavia, was a film that nearly cost Jackie his life when he slipped from a tree and fell onto a pile of rocks below, sustaining a serious head injury.

documentary, which I've just finished. Everybody has seen different documentaries that have been made about me—OK, now I'll make my own documentary that I want you to see. That's how I like to do it. It's not, "Let's make ten movies this year," or "Let's make ten or fifteen million dollars"—no. I want to make something interesting—like, if James Cameron or Steven Spielberg called me up and said, "Jackie we want you to make a movie with us for free"—I'd bring my own money, I'd bring my own lunch! Because I want to learn something. I want to learn how they can make 100-million- or 200-million-dollar movies. How can they make that boat—the *Titanic*—look so real?

What, to date, has been your favorite movie of yours?

If you're talking about action, I think *Police Story.*

Why is that?

Because it was the first time I changed the action sequence, the fighting style. Almost everybody, even my stuntmen and myself, really risked our lives. We put our lives on the line to really do some dangerous stunts. A lot of people got hurt. And the movie, when it was released, all of Asia went wild for it. Even in America, when it came out on video, the people went crazy over it.

What has been your favorite movie that you've directed so far?

Well, if you are talking about director skill, technique—it would have to be *Miracles,* or as it is also known, *Mr. Canton and Lady Rose,* which I did in 1989.

What has been your favorite fight sequence that you've coordinated?

I like certain parts from every movie I've made. Like the end fighting scene from *Drunken Master II,* and the fight in the park at night from *Police Story II.* I like a lot of things. Even now when I watch old films of myself, the old days, I'm surprised, too. I say, "That's me?" I've done so many things, some-

Whenever Jackie does his acrobatics, he always keeps the action within the realm of probability. He recalls, "When I went to a film festival in Paris two years ago, so many people asked me, 'Why is it that in Hong Kong films everybody can fly?' It's very stupid! When I watch a lot of Hong Kong films, I don't know what the hell is going on."

times even I forget what I've done. And when I finally get a chance to look at these films, I go "Wow! I really did do a lot of good things."

The fight choreography in **Drunken Master II** *was crisp and clear. After so many kung-fu and swordplay movies where everyone is flying around and the action was made up of rapid cuts, which was very confusing to the audience, your action was stylized but still realistic. You used wires a few times but simply to enhance the action.*

[laughing] Exactly! That's why I spent such a long time on the action for this film. Too often Hong Kong films go crazy with the action sequences. When I went to a film festival in Paris two years ago, so many people asked me, "Why is it that in Hong Kong films everybody can fly?" It's very stupid! When I watch a lot of Hong Kong films, I don't know what the hell is going on. It's all quick cuts and moves that are too fast. All the action is doubles—not stunt but body doubles! When the actor comes onto the set, it's just for one or two hours, and they just sit down and do close-ups. Or like this, [mimes harp playing, dispatching darts against numerous enemies] then you cut to explosions and stuntmen reacting. I see this kind of action and wonder why they didn't use these weapons in the Gulf War! [laughing] It's stupid! And even more crazy is the fact that even though everyone can fly, they ride horses. I look at this kind of film and I really think people overseas will think Hong Kong films are rubbish. For a long time I had wanted to make *Drunken Master II*, and when there was the return of the kung-fu movie I thought that it was time. But when we were making the film, many other kung-fu movies were failing at the box office and people told me that I was too late and missed the boat. But I think it's not too late if I make a good film, then the audiences will come to see it. (JC/PNP)

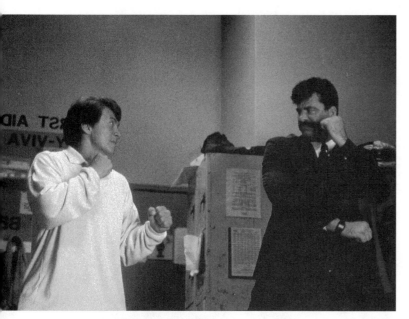

Jackie squares off against yet another heavy—just prior to his famous shark-tank encounter—in the film *First Strike*.

You proved that with Drunken Master II's success. I was surprised that nobody has tried to copy its style of action since its release.

They want to! I am not the best action actor in Asia, but I am lucky for two reasons. One is that I love making movies, so I take a lot of care to produce good ones; two, I also have Raymond Chow and Golden Harvest behind me and willing to support me. You know that, just for the last scene in the foundry, we spent a couple of months! Many companies do not have the time to spend on getting things just right, they have to rush their productions out. For me, I'm lucky that I have support, that I can spend one day for one shot. [laughing] I'm not young anymore—I can jump about six feet in the air but only for a few takes. After five to six takes I can't jump that high anymore, so I stop and do some other shots. The next day I will try again to do that movement. But many companies haven't got the time or money—they have to finish that shot today. So often they will do a stupid wire shot that's unbelievable just to get the shot, and that's why they too often end up with bad movies. I know a lot of other action actors who are very, very good, but they don't have the time or the money to make their action [scenes] as good as mine. Maybe they had only three days to film the whole fight scene. (JC/PNP)

I remember being on one set and everyone was rushing to finish the film that night, because it was previewing five days later.

You know it! The quality of a film is very important. After we finished *Rumble in the Bronx*, we took it to Australia to do the Dolby sound and then to America for the music. We try to make it the very best we can, but I think some local companies try to make their films the very worst they can! They destroy themselves. Right now, Hong Kong films are losing in Hong Kong to Western films for the second year running, and the whole market in Asia for Hong Kong films is very bad. Even the big films like Chow Yun-Fat's *God of Gamblers 2/God of Gamblers Returns* and Jet Li's *Fist of Legend* are not doing well in other countries—even in Korea![9] Also, while Gordon Chan Kar Sang is very good at directing drama, Yuen Woo Ping is in complete control for the action scenes. So when there is an action scene, Gordon isn't there and Yuen Woo Ping takes over. After the action is completed, maybe a couple of days later, Gordon comes back. That's why there is a bad mixture between the tone of the film's drama and action scenes. That's wrong. On my films, no matter who the director is, I will spend as much time as

In *Rumble in the Bronx*, Jackie was extensively involved in all aspects of the production. He even claimed that at times he was on the set even more than the director!

possible on the set. From my experience, I have found that really no one can direct me by themselves. On *Crime Story* and *Rumble in the Bronx*, I was always on the set, sometimes even more than the director! I am almost the co-director of the film. If the film does badly it reflects upon me, so I try and take care of my career. (JC/PNP)

If you look at the Hong Kong film industry of the last ten years, you seem to be the only really stable figure, so your strategy obviously works.

[shakes his head] You know that everybody says to me, "Jackie, you're a miracle! You are still at the top, your films are still making money, how do you do this?" I tell them that I'm not a miracle, it's just that I care about my career. There's one action actor that I know, he's very successful, but now he seems to be losing his appeal. One time he was actually filming two action films at Golden Harvest at the same time. One day he is meant to be filming two major action scenes, one for each film, and what does he do? He comes into my office and starts telling me that he is tired and ends up sleeping on my couch! I went to both stages and he had stunt doubles doing all his

Jackie mirrors his foe in a back alley scene from *Mr. Nice Guy*, which was shot in Melbourne, Australia.

action. I went back to my office and talked to him. He told me that there's no need for either him or me to do all the fighting or dangerous stunts in our films—we can just let the stuntmen do it. I wondered if he was right, but then both of his films failed at the box office. And then I knew that I was right—you have to take care of your film. And not just for the Hong Kong and Taiwanese markets, but for the rest of the markets.

I always tell my crew, it's bad if you lie to other people but it's stupid if you lie to yourself. If you tell the truth, maybe people won't always like what you say, but they will believe it and respect you. That's my philosophy; if someone asks me a question I tell them the truth, how I feel. It's like yesterday, I was told that I am going to receive an award for "Best Asian Actor" at some ceremony. The newspapers ask me how I feel and I tell them the truth. If I am getting an award I feel very happy but especially if it's an award that means something. In Hong Kong it's strange. There are four radio stations and they all have separate awards ceremonies—which is OK—but they give awards to everybody! It's stupid. I give an award to you, then so your photographer doesn't feel sad, I give him an award too, and then I give myself one—it's worthless. If I was to win an Academy Award, an Oscar, of course I will be happy and feel very proud, because there is only one Oscar. So it's very special. It means something. But if L.A. had an Oscar, and New York had an Oscar, and Chicago, then nobody would care. Give people an award that means something! (JC/PNP)

Another thing Drunken Master II *proved was that, beyond a doubt, you are still in incredible physical condition, and can still perform some incredible martial artistry. In the West, a lot of people had cited the lack of lengthy fight scenes in films like* Police Story III *and* Crime Story *as proof that you were trying to get away from the martial arts action as you get older.* Drunken Master II *certainly silenced those critics. Did you have to do a lot of special martial arts training to get back into form?*

[laughing] Yes! I did a lot of training for *Drunken Master II*, and that's one of the reasons that I didn't want to direct the film. But when I say I don't want to direct, it doesn't mean that I will have no input or say-so regarding the film. But having someone else direct means I can spend more time training, and perhaps even have a social life! [laughing] When I am directing on my own, I take control of casting, locations, sound track, the editing, everything. And it takes about two years to do each film. With training, it

Dean Shek (left) attempts
to teach Jackie's (right)
character the importance
of concentration in
Drunken Master.

all depends upon the movie; its time, setting, and the style; if it's dramatic
or comical. If I'm doing *Drunken Master III*, then, of course, I will spend a
lot of time training in traditional kung fu. You know, I have my own ideas
concerning *Drunken Master III*—not Lau Chia Liang's one, but a proper
sequel. The reaction from people around the world tells me that there is still
a market that wants to see *Drunken Master*–style films. But I'm still working
on a story line that's different. If you look at the original *Drunken Master*
with Yuen Woo Ping, the story is very simple—just drinking, fighting, and
comedy. There isn't much depth to it. For *Part II*, we gave the audience a
more adult story line that you shouldn't drink too much and mixed it in with
a story about stolen treasure. But for *Part III*, I still haven't got a good story
line finished, but of course when it comes to filming it, I will start training
like this again. [starts humming Wong Fei Hung music and doing drunken
boxing]

Jackie on the receiving end of some fancy footwork in 1980's *Young Master*. This film established Jackie as a bona fide superstar, allowing him to take home a million-dollar paycheck.

I watch a lot of modern-day Hong Kong films and people are driving cars and firing guns, but when they fight they do this! [Jackie adopts choy lee fut and wushu poses] It's stupid! Just like the old kung-fu movies. [laughing] In a modern film, the action should be more rough and ready, like this. [Jackie starts throwing punches and kicks] You know when I made *Operation Condor*, I had to fight a lot of Western actors and stuntmen. Bruce Fontaine and Kenn Goodman really are two of the best Western martial artists I have worked with, because they are very versatile and are two of the very few I have met who can handle Hong Kong action. But I had to tell them that they were not playing martial artists but mercenaries with only basic training. They can both do very good Chinese martial arts, including a lot of acrobatic moves, but I wanted them to look rough—more like street fighters than very graceful martial artists. When I watch a modern-day film, and people are fighting with very traditional kung-fu movements, it just doesn't make sense. The problem is often due to the fight choreographer—on a lot of films, the director will leave the handling of the action scenes entirely to the action director/fight choreographer. This can lead to a lot of problems because the action director might not realize that a scene should be very serious and maybe choreographs a lighthearted fight scene or something that doesn't match the tone of the film, and the director comes back only after the action is finished, maybe a couple of days later. By the time they realize that the fight scene doesn't match the rest of the film's style, it's too late to change it. That's why I work very closely with the director on most aspects of the film. (JC/PNP)

That's probably why all of your films have a very steady, even feel to them. The action flows with the story.

I take care because everything I have now is a result of my movies! If my movie fails then no audience, no money, no fans, no business. That's why I take care. "Movies are my life!" (JC/PNP)

Jackie (left) and Ken Lo (right) are good friends in real life but staged one of the greatest kung-fu fights ever filmed in Jackie's *Drunken Master II*.

I was very surprised that while Michael Ho Sung Pak (Lu K'ang of Mortal Kombat video game fame) worked on Drunken Master II for so long, he didn't really do anything. When I spoke to him on the set he told me that he was finding Hong Kong choreography difficult to relate to, and in the finished film he is doubled for some of his action by Wong Ming Sang.

[nodding] Yes, actually I didn't know Michael Ho—he was playing one of the *Teenage Mutant Ninja Turtles* when Lau Chia Liang, who was working on *TMNT 3*, invited him to Hong Kong and gave him a major role in *Drunken Master II*. I didn't doubt Lau Chia Liang's judgment, so I didn't ask to see what he could do or give him any special training. We were saving him for the end of the film to have the big fight. After Lau Chia Liang left the project we were ready to shoot the end scene and it was a mistake. For Hong Kong fighting there is a rhythm, it's not just one or two moves and then the cut—we have a lot of continuous action. Ho Sung Pak just couldn't catch the rhythm. It doesn't mean that he isn't a very good martial artist; he just couldn't get into the rhythm, couldn't catch the flavor. So I changed the ending to just a few

moves and Michael is finished. Then I go on and fight Ken Lo Wai Kwong. I told Ken to work on getting as flexible as possible so that we can have a wild fight scene. So for one month, Ken is doing the splits everyday, everywhere, [laughing] even when he is sleeping! You look at the end fight scene, forget Jean-Claude Van Damme, Ken shows what kicking is! (JC/PNP)

I know that a lot of footage was removed from Drunken Master II *before release. In the West there is now a growing trend in releasing "director's cuts" of films, with reinstated footage. Would you want to release a revised version of* Drunken Master II*?*

No, I only take out footage if it doesn't work, so to put any footage back would make the film worse. A lot of the footage that we cut was Lau Chia Liang's interpretation of Joy Kun/Drunken Boxing. He doesn't like [my] drunken boxing, he wants it to be like real kung fu. In his mind, drunken kung fu is like this, [Jackie demonstrates one drunken movement before dropping back to normal] somebody hits you, then you are drunk for just one movement, then back to normal. I know that my version of drunken boxing is not real kung fu, but the real thing is boring and doesn't look good on film, while my version looks good. That's why we had to reshoot so many scenes because Lau Chia Liang's views and mine are very different. You know the scene at the end when I read the message on the fan? Well, we had already filmed the scene where I fight Vincent Tuatane with the fan, and we couldn't reshoot it. So we spent a lot of time thinking of a reason why I would have the fan, and then I can think, "If it has a message on it that inspires me to change my strategy, then I can use it!" And after I finished the reshoots on *Drunken Master II* and showed it to the HKSA, they gave me a standing ovation. I am very happy that they and the audience are happy with the film. (JC/PNP)

Prior to Drunken Master II*, you made the dark-edged drama,* Crime Story, *for Kirk Wong. The film really gave you a chance to stretch your*

In *Armor of God*, Jackie plays the Asian Hawk, an Indiana Jones–style adventurer who uses all means at his disposal to rescue his ex-girlfriend.

acting skills. Your character is haunted by inner demons and both attracted to and repelled by the violence he encounters. How did you first get involved with this film?

When I was filming *Twin Dragons*, with Kirk Wong playing the main bad guy, he was telling me how he wanted to make this police drama about a real kidnapping case in Hong Kong a few years ago. It sounded very interesting, but at that time I had no room in my schedule and also he was just about to begin a production with Jet Li in the lead. A few months later, I saw Kirk at Golden Harvest and he looked very depressed. He told me that he was having a lot of problems with the production and that Jet Li had walked off the film and now production was going to stop. I said to him and my production crew that I wanted to take over the lead and complete the film, but due to my schedule we would have to film the movie in between other projects. So we started working and that's why it took so long to complete. (JC/PNP)

"The fighting and stunts are getting more and more difficult now; each film I have to try and top the previous one."—Jackie Chan

You took a big risk with such a dramatic role. Although the film was a box-office smash, your performance was vindicated when you won your second Golden Horse Award as "Best Actor" for the film. Did you find it more difficult to play such a serious role?

No, it's much easier because I was just the actor, and [laughing] not too much fighting; it wasn't as painful. The fighting and stunts are getting more and more difficult now; each film I have to try and top the previous one. I don't think there is anyone left to fight anymore. I have fought Sammo Hung, Dick Wei, Benny Urquidez, Bill Wallace, and Lo Wai Kwong. The audience wants me to fight someone new, but who? (JC/PNP)

*Maybe you should fight the dinosaurs from **Jurassic Park**?*

Maybe. Yes, something that isn't human, maybe something half-human and half-monster. That would be an interesting fight. But it's very difficult always fighting; acting is much easier! (JC/PNP)

Once again a lot of scenes were cut from **Crime Story,** *including a lot of scenes with Singaporean actress Christine Ng, who played your doctor. She was in town for a long time but is in the film only for a little while. What happened?*

[laughing] You know too much! It's very difficult to say what happened. I like Kirk Wong and his style of filmmaking, but, well, he wants to do a lot of things in the film and he doesn't always know how to do it! A lot of scenes with me and Christine were very strange, they didn't make sense. Kirk has a very New Wave style of directing but I don't think his style and mine work well together. (JC/PNP)

Before **Crime Story,** *you teamed up with director Wong Jing (*God of Gamblers*) for the live-action adaptation of the Japanese animated series* **City Hunter.** *This was a film that seemed to have all the various elements of a classic, but the film turned out to be a disappointment.*

"If you make a good, strong film, then you have the chance to make a sequel. That's why I try to take care of my career. You should look at your work like an investment; take care of it and it takes care of you."—Jackie Chan

I agree, the film was not very good. It made money only because at that time the *City Hunter* comics and animated series were very popular throughout Asia, so the film had a built-in audience. But I am very disappointed with the film and I know that the audience feels the same way. (JC/PNP)

Do you think that it might have been another case where your style and Wong Jing's style clashed? You are very much a perfectionist, while Wong Jing is by his own admission a purely commercial director; he doesn't want critical success, merely box-office success.

[laughing] Yes, I think that you could be right. I didn't find it difficult working with Wong Jing; he was one of the easiest to work with. As you said, he doesn't mind if you want to change things. If I say to him, "Can I change this part?" He says, "No problem." If I ask him, "Can I direct this part?" he would say, "Of course, go ahead!" It's funny, but a lot of the time he wasn't on the set, because he had several projects going at the same time. Sometimes I'm not on the set, he's not on the set, and it's just his assistant director doing the work. (JC/PNP)

Project A is considered a unique film—even for Jackie Chan—on many levels, full of death-defying stunts, good music, terrific sets, and comedy.

The City Hunter *concept had been such a great success as a comic book and animated series. But despite the film having so many elements from the original, it just didn't seem to mix.*

[nodding his head] I know, I was disappointed myself. Wong Jing is very commercial, and his films do well at the box office but his style is too loose for me. People were expecting great things when Wong Jing and I teamed up, but everybody was disappointed. (JC/PNP)

When you announced the project, you said that it would be the first in a series of City Hunter *films. You wanted it to be a series of James Bond–flavored action comedies.*

If I had directed *City Hunter*, right now we would be making a sequel to it. At first Golden Harvest was very happy with the film, because it came in on schedule and under budget, and did quite well at the box office. But now they realize that the market won't accept a further *City Hunter* film because the audience felt so disappointed. Most of the films I have directed, we have been able to make sequels to because both the audience and the box-office takings have called for them. In the next couple of years I can make *Armor of God III*, *Project A III*, or *Police Story IX* if I want to. If you make a good, strong film, then you have the chance to make a sequel. That's why I try to take care of my career. You should look at your work like an investment; take care of it and it takes care of you. (JC/PNP)

In 1993 you turned up in a very interesting cameo in Stanley Tong's Project S/Once a Cop. You don't normally do cameos; why this one?

I like Stanley, he's a good friend and a very good director. I did the cameo to help him. If I'm in the film it is easier for him to sell it, [laughing] even if I'm in drag! Also, I am on the board at Golden Harvest, so I am helping my own company. If the film doesn't do well, then there will be problems for me when I want to make my next movie. I want to work with Stanley but if the film is a flop, Golden Harvest won't want me to. So I did the cameo and they put me on the poster, and while the film wasn't a huge success it did reasonably well. (JC/PNP)

Crime Story (1993) was based on the true story of a businessman who was kidnapped twice and held for a ransom of $6 million. Jackie plays the police detective in charge of the case.

In the past few years, you have announced several projects that have yet to be made. Could you comment on their status? Starting with **Singapore Sling,** *Golden Harvest's proposed action comedy for the international market that was announced five years ago.*

Even megahits like *Rumble in the Bronx* are heavily edited by the American production companies. Jackie says, "The editors thought it was much simpler to just cut everything that was dialogue, which makes me ashamed. I really hope that one day I can direct here, and then nobody can cut my film."

That one! Golden Harvest wanted me to do another American film but one that was more of an action comedy. They were throwing names like Tom Hanks and Chevy Chase around as costars. But nothing was ever confirmed, and truthfully I don't want to make any more American films because the two I've done before, *The Big Brawl* and *The Protector*, not only didn't do too well in Asia, they were also a failure at the American box office. Western audiences seem to like my Hong Kong films better then my American ones, so for now I make my films as Hong Kong international films. (JC/PNP)

Fireman's Story *is one project that I know you have been wanting to do for a very long time. In 1991 the film was announced as going into production with Buddhist Fist as star and Tsui Siu Ming as director. The film was to feature little fighting, a lot of drama and emotion, and some incredible fire stunts. I've spoken with both top Hong Kong cinematographer Peter Pau (***Misty, Saviour of the Soul***) and your former assistant director P'ng Kialek about the film, and both told me how the special-effects crew from* **Backdraft** *were attached to the project and that several incredible fire sequences had been planned. What is the status of the film?*

I'll make it one day. You know, we have already spent several million Hong Kong dollars on the film's preproduction. I first had the idea a long time ago, and when I saw Ron Howard's movie I knew that we could do the special effects we needed, but it will be bigger than *Backdraft*. Then just when we were ready to begin production, ATV (Hong Kong's second TV channel) made a drama series called *Flame* about the firemen. So I put the film on the back burner. I know that one day I will make it. I like the script and the emotion in the story. (JC/PNP)

What about your Eastern Western?

It's going to be made. You know I had the idea for *Rumble in the Bronx* several years ago. So many times I get ready to start one of these films and then something happens and I end up doing another project. (JC/PNP)

In the future, would you like to be doing more hands-on directing so that you can take more control of the story and present it in the way you would like to see it done?

"The most important thing I always tell myself and tell my boys is, 'You can lie to the audience, but don't lie to yourself.' When I'm making a movie, it is not first for the audience, it is first for myself. When I can look at it and like it, then I'll present it to the audience. That's when I can say to them, 'That's my movie, that's a Jackie Chan movie.'"—Jackie Chan

Yes, I will do more directing, but it's difficult—especially in Asia—no matter how well you direct, they do not respect you. The countries, like Taiwan, Thailand, the Philippines, they do not respect you. They will just cut the dialogue and make everything just fighting. They don't care about the dialogue, they only care about the fighting. So it makes the story not work. When I look at American movies, the drama, the stories, are the best. The fighting they don't give much attention to, just one punch, two punch. I want a good story, a good drama, and good fighting. But my films always end up getting cut—they make my movie look like crap—just fighting, fighting,

fighting, fighting, fighting. Even when my movies come to America, the American production company does the same thing. They just cut the comedy things, cut the drama things. All you see in Jackie Chan films is fighting, fighting, fighting, fighting.

So how can you control that more?

I'm not sure. Because if James Cameron made *Titanic* in Asia, I don't think the result would have been that good, because they would have cut it. But now American directors are so powerful in this country that they can say, "You cannot cut my version—that's my version. I'll sue you." Soon other countries learn that if you try to alter an American movie, they can sue you and you lose money. So that way, they cannot touch you. With Hong Kong directors, we're not as powerful as American directors, so we're not going to sue you. And, after all those years, we've just gotten used to it. Like for fifteen or twenty years, we just let them cut our films. The Hong Kong filmmakers are used to having their films cut. Besides, Chinese is not the national language. In America, everybody is used to listening to American English, so when our movies—which were originally shot in Chinese—were released in this country, it was all dubbing, dubbing, dubbing, dubbing. So the editors thought it was much simpler to just cut everything that was dialogue, which makes me ashamed. I really hope that one day I can direct here, and then nobody can cut my film. Even though I am famous now, they will still cut a half hour from my film.

"On my films, no matter who the director is, I will spend as much time as possible on the set."—Jackie Chan

That's awful, but it leads to my next question. You are an artist in what you do—not only in acting, but in choreography and in directing. And, like a great painter, you understandably don't want people messing with your artwork. I'd like to ask you what is your definition of an "artist."

Like I said before, you are the one saying that I am an artist. A lot of people say, "Aw, you are an artist." I don't know. Who am I? I just know what I am doing. That's the way I'm making a movie. I just know that I'm making the

Chan is so artistic in his cinematic presentation of martial arts that some have dubbed him the "Baryshnikov of Battery."

kind of movie I like to make and that my character is speaking the kind of dialogue that I want. Yes. A lot of people ask me, "What is your motivation for this? What is your philosophy of filmmaking?" I just know that if I want this tight shot, I just have to move the camera this way—and I just know how to do it. That's the way that Jackie Chan films. Jackie Chan's idea is the film, but I just don't know if what you said about me is really me. I don't know if I am an artist or not. If you say I am an artist, I thank you. If you say I am a moneymaker, OK. If you don't like my movie, sorry. The most important thing I always tell myself and tell my boys is, "You can lie to the audience, but don't lie to yourself." When I'm making a movie, it is not first for the audience, it is first for myself. When I can look at it and like it, then I'll present it to the audience. That's when I can say to them, "That's my movie, that's a Jackie Chan movie." If I don't like the movie, I'll never do promotion for it. How could I tell the audience to go and see something that I thought was terrible? No way!

What are your feelings about the movie you're presently working on,* Rush Hour*? Are you happy with it, or not?

I'm happy I'm filming an American movie, but I'm not happy to be under the restraints of the American [production] system. However, I want to learn the American system, so that's why I've come to America to make this movie. I tell myself, "This time I'm coming to America to be in school— three months. No harm." It's three months for me to learn what the system is. Learn why they have such great budgets, how they work on the sets. Why they have so many cameras, so many people on the set. I just want to learn. But when I come here this time, I'm still not used to it. They have so many people; they have a director, they have a camera director, they have an editing director, they have music—too many directors. The producer is the most powerful, and also the first A.D. [assistant director], who can say, "You have to go to lunch now." "Why?" "No, you have to go." So everybody has lunch, then it's a wrap, and everybody goes home. For now, I'm still not used to it, but I'm learning. Until the movie is finished, I have no way of knowing how it will turn out. I will wait for the audience to tell me either, "No, Jackie, we like your style. We don't like the way you are making American movies." That way I can change. Either way I'll learn something though. Ultimately it doesn't matter.

On Fight Scene
Choreography

There is something magical about a Jackie Chan fight scene. It is a spellbinding mixture of action/fantasy and martial realism that comes across the screen. Jackie's fight sequences take on a life of their own and draw the audience into them, so much so, in fact, that the audiences tend to heave a sigh of relief—along with Jackie—when he finally emerges triumphant.

Apart from being a talented martial artist himself, which allows him to perform virtually any combative technique, Jackie is also a superb athlete. This further broadens the scope of his options and improvisational abilities in his fighting sequences. And then there is the fact that during the last twenty years, Jackie has worked alongside all of the big names in martial arts and martial arts movies. He was a stuntman for the late Bruce Lee during two of Lee's pictures that were filmed in Hong Kong and, undoubtedly, watched and learned how Lee went about setting up his own phenomenal action sequences. Later, Jackie worked with Sammo Hung, who was not only his "older brother" from his Peking Opera days but also one of the top stunt coordinators in Southeast Asia. But being an artist himself, Jackie has created his own unique action and comedy twists to the genre of fight choreography, putting his own personal and unique stamp on every fight sequence he performs. And he's showing absolutely no signs of slowing down, which is quite an accomplishment when you consider the fact that Jackie's been mixing it up with some of the very best fighters in the world for well over two decades now.

Jackie, you have fought a lot of Western martial arts actors in your films, including Bill "Superfoot" Wallace, Benny Urquidez, Keith Vimli, Richard Norton, and Gary Daniels. While in your films they have looked good, when they return to the West and make films, they never look as effective. Why do you think this is?

When it comes to fight scene choreography, Jackie Chan is in a class of his own. Here he lets his feet do the talking in an on-screen battle from *Police Story*.

Choreography! Action or martial arts choreography is so important. The camera angles, the editing, the tempo of the fight, all of these things are very important. In real life you can be the greatest martial artist or greatest street fighter of all time, but if you have poor choreography, editing—or if you don't understand how to put together a cinematic fight scene—you aren't going to look that good. In Hong Kong, all the action directors have a wide knowledge of different martial arts, camera angles, film speed, editing techniques, and so on. I know these things myself, because I've been making films for most of my life. You can't just pick it up overnight. In America, they have the best special effects, the best computer effects, the best mechanical effects, while here in Hong Kong, our special effects are very basic. But for fight scenes, the U.S. is still far behind us. They don't understand how to film a fight. I've worked in America and visited many film sets.

But so many times, the action director on an American film won't even look through the camera, let alone edit the scene himself. That's not good, you have to have an editor who understands the tempo, who knows how to put a fight scene together. But if he didn't choreograph it, he isn't going to understand how to bring it together in the editing room. (JC/PNP)

Jackie's training in classical martial art techniques served him well during his fight sequences for *Young Master.*

What are your thoughts on the martial arts you see performed in the movies these days by other actors?

Right now, in the movies, they don't really utilize martial arts anymore. Not classical martial arts, anyway. It's action, action—it's more than simply fighting these days. It's more like boxing. Even the kicking is different. And also, right now too many people are kicking in the movies. So I don't want to kick. I want to make myself special. Van Damme is kicking, everybody is kicking—that's the big thing, apparently. So I want to make my movies different, so I'm not kicking so much. I do more difficult things, like jumping on the sofa and going up to the roof. I do so many different things, like punching with a bicycle, or I'll flip kick with a motorcycle. I want to

In *Rumble in the Bronx*, Jackie demonstrated how a ski can make a formidable weapon—in the hands of someone who knows how to employ it.

Fans from all over the world flock to Jackie whenever they spot him. Here he poses for a photo with two fans during a visit to Beverly Hills.

use some other thing, not just stand there and fight—boom! Or throw high kicks.

One thing I do notice is that you make your fight scenes practical. For example, if there is something on a table that you can use to help yourself out of a jam, then you incorporate it into your fight scene, rather than the typical North American method of simply "putting up your dukes" and delivering a punch toward the camera, and then cutting the scene to show a close-up of an adversary taking the punch on the jaw. This is important because, while you still perform your incredible feats of skill and martial arts mastery, you remain believable to the audience. Is this something that you've deliberately intended to infuse into your fight scenes, or is it something that just happened to evolve over time?

I just don't know. I went to the video store the other day to look at something, and I was shocked at how many "biographies" there are on me! [laughs] There's too many. But seeing the boxes and, later, looking at my older movies, like, the ones I did twenty-five or thirty years ago, it's almost like looking at a different person. I was almost pure classical kung fu in my moves, doing techniques from different martial art styles. There would be no use, for example, of chairs in my fight scenes, or other props, just hand-to-hand fighting in a very traditional manner.

How do you go about setting up your fight sequences? What's the most difficult aspect of your choreography?

For a stunt coordinator to choreograph all the fighting scenes, the most difficult thing is the initiation of the fight between two people—how do you

A small cart gives Jackie the leverage he needs to put some extra thrust into his side kick, as he dispatches his opponent in *First Strike*.

"You must put both the thought process and emotion of the character into the fight sequence, particularly at the initiation of the fight."
—Jackie Chan

land the first punch? That's very difficult. Then you think about what are the reasons why the character is going to fight? What are his motivations for throwing that first punch? Then, when you start that first punch and kicking, it becomes very easy in terms of what camera angles to use, and things like that. When do the combatants separate? Catch their breath? And then resume fighting? And then, what are the strikes or kicks that would be suitable for them at this juncture of the fight?

Many things have to be considered when choreographing a fight scene, besides simply a string of techniques, because we are not two gentlemen fighting [adopts a John L. Sullivan pose] where it's [adopts a polite expression]: "Okay, now we will fight." That's not how fights take place in these days. It's more like, "You kill my sister, I'll kill your father! Aaaagh!" [jumps up and delivers several lightning-fast strikes] As the fighter, you would have to think about going there ahead of time to fight this person, and once there you would look for something—anything—to get it going. If you saw a table, you probably would kick it toward your opponent, because then it might hit him and hurt him, or, at the very least, it would distract his attention so that you could close the gap between the two of you with a technique— boom! [throws a backfist at an imaginary opponent] You make some move, or think about "How can I make that first contact?" That's important. You must put both the thought process and emotion of the character into the fight sequence, particularly at the initiation of the fight.

So, this is the way that I choreograph my fight scenes. It's a mixture of things. It's not like, "OK, I don't like you. You don't like me. So now we'll go outside and have a fight. Come on. Now, are you ready? [puts up his hands in a fighting posture] Yes, now I am ready—Boom! boom! boom! [simulates punches being thrown,

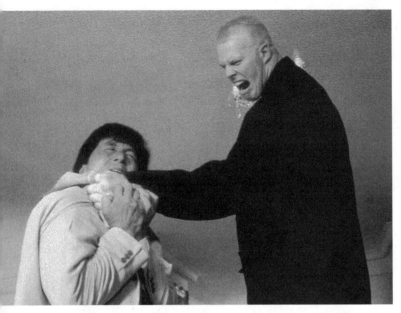

When all else fails—bite! Jackie using whatever weapon is available to him during action from *First Strike*.

"When I am teaching people fighting I am also teaching them the emotions and motivation behind their actions."— Jackie Chan.

then steps back into his fighting stance once more] Now, let's do it again." That's a different kind of thing. The way I choreograph fight scenes was actually a big help to me in becoming a good director, because when I teach people fighting I am also teaching them the emotions and motivation behind their actions, like, why I'm kicking the table, why I'm doing this, why I'm doing that. So later on, my martial art choreography changed from pure martial arts to action. Right now, it's the twentieth century, almost the twenty-first century—how can you justify fighting in this way? No, it's ridiculous. Getting into classical, traditional kung-fu stances and gentleman-style techniques is OK for comedy. [throws a series of wild-man punches and then quickly attempts to adopt a classical kung-fu stance in order to make it look like the previous punches were part of his style and not simply wild swinging] It's not like before, though. I'm the one who really wants to change these types of things and make the fight choreography more up to date and modern. You see this in not only martial arts, but with dancing, with the rhythm and everything.

You must notice a huge difference between your approach and that of your American counterparts in the film world.

A lot of American movies feature fighting that is really just old-time martial art. [assumes several classical and theatrical fighting stances and techniques] And that's wrong. Now, of course there is an audience for this type of fighting, but it's small. Only a small number of people make up that type of audience. Most audiences like to see the real thing, not the old traditional thing. They like the natural thing—the way fighting really is—natural comedy, too.

"Most audiences like to see the real thing, not the old traditional thing. They like the natural thing—the way fighting really is—natural comedy, too."—Jackie Chan

You mentioned that when you kick a table, for example, toward an opponent to initiate a fight, it brings a lot of emotion into your fight scenes, whereas a Jean-Claude Van Damme, for example, seems to prefer using orthodox martial arts kicking, which many filmgoers find unbelievable.

I think every action star—not only Van Damme—Stallone, Chuck Norris, whoever, are good fighters and martial artists. Or if not good fighters, at least good actors. The only reason that Jackie Chan has become special is because they don't know how to choreograph, they only know how to fight. And when they make an action movie, maybe their director is not a martial artist, he is only the director. Which means that when they fight, everything's wrong. So this way, when the action in the movie comes up, it doesn't make sense sometimes. It doesn't look as good as a Jackie Chan movie. Why? Because when I direct all the fighting scenes, I'm directing myself. And, most important, I use my own stuntmen. Even if I were making a movie where you were the director, when it came time to film the fight scene, you would go away and I would direct it. So this way, it makes my action movie more exciting than some other people's. This doesn't mean

Jackie in *Project A:* "When you look at Jackie Chan's action, it works."

that I am better than Van Damme—no, because Van Damme is good. But because of the situation, the people here in America have to listen to one person tell them how to fight. Then if the actor wants to do this type of kick but his stuntman doesn't know how to do the proper reaction, and the cameraman, who is a good photographer but is unfamiliar with how to ideally film action scenes, and the director is more drama-oriented than action-oriented—all of these things combine to make the action scene not work. When you look at Jackie Chan's action, it works. Why? Because I use my own cameraman, my own lighting man, my own stuntman; I'm the director, I'm the stunt coordinator, I'm the actor! So I do everything.

You are able to tell a story with your choreography. Most people in the West simply punch toward the camera and then cut to a reaction shot of the opponent going back, but you actually tell a story through your choreography. That's a real art.

Why, when I'm fighting, do the people care more? Because I'm the director. How can I say it? I just don't understand why in America, when they do a movie like *Jurassic Park*, they did [part] in California, they did the sound track for another dinosaur in New York and the big-foot dinosaur tight shot in Pittsburgh. They're separate. And when they do the special effects, they have five teams and, later on, they combine it all together. Sometimes when I watch a lot of Asian fighting scenes in Hong Kong, the director is a good director but he doesn't know how to fight. When he does the dialogue scenes, the stunt coordinator isn't there. Maybe he's out fooling around, maybe he's off watching another movie. Big stunt coordinators are always busy, maybe filming five or ten movies at the same time. They don't have time to create the different actions that would be appropriate for each character. Instead, they go to movie "A" and tell the people to do "three punches and one kick." Then they go to movie "B" and tell them "three punches, one kick." Then they go to another movie set and tell them "three punches, one kick." All the same thing because they don't have the time to create new things. And when the director shoots the dialogue/drama scene, he calls in the stunt coordinator. He comes in and says, "Action! Chris Tucker fights Jackie, Jackie beats him up and then leaves. Two punches, one kick."

"Even if I were making a movie where you were the director, when it came time to film the fight scene, you would go away and I would direct it."
—Jackie Chan

"Even fighting has a
drama."—Jackie Chan

Finished. When the movie is finished and you see this, it leaves you flat,
because even fighting has a drama. But this does not have a drama.

*When you are as creative as you are, and you know from experience what
makes for a spectacular and successful fight sequence and what makes the
audience really enjoy a movie, does it frustrate you to come here and work
with American directors who don't have the same knowledge and feel for the
action as you do?*

Yeah, it kind of makes me frustrated. And also, sometimes when it's not my
business I want to tell the director, "You should do that for this character."
What kind of fighting you do depends on the type of character you are
playing. Like in this movie I'm shooting now [*Rush Hour*], Chris Tucker's
character fighting is more comedy. My kind of fighting should be like a James
Dean fighting—pow! pow!—you know, clean and precise. Sharp. Then you
have comedy. What kind of character's fighting is the most serious? The bad
guy. You cannot tell sometimes when I see an American movie, everybody is
kicking! It takes away from the power of the actor when he kicks. If the

Jackie employs a foot-sweep technique during his bare-knuckle tournament fight in *The Big Brawl*.

actor is going to kick, OK, then let this guy just punch, and let this other guy do different things. You have to create a lot of different things. When I direct, I cannot direct unless I'm on the set and can tell the actor, "When you start fighting, this is the kind of punch you need."

On Stunt Coordinating

His combination of humor and death-defying stunts defines a style that Jackie Chan invented at the beginning of the 1980s and carried to extravagant heights—a style that American films are only now attempting. Los Angeles–based film writer Manohla Dargis noted recently, "Nearly a decade before James Cameron had actors hanging off flying machines in *True Lies* (courtesy of blue screens, mind you), Asia's answer to Arnold Schwarzenegger was swinging off a hot-air balloon in *Armor of God*."

A defier of death, Chan nearly lost his life when he took an unscheduled forty-five-foot fall in *Armor of God*. Among other close calls, he was sideswiped by a helicopter while hanging from a train in *Police Story III*. A superb martial artist and acrobat, Jackie has built his legend by putting his life on the line for his movies. The *New York Times* noted that "For more than twenty years he has refused to let a stuntman fill in for him during dangerous scenes." Fans see the proof of this in the montage of outtakes that typically ends his films. Jackie Chan, in other words, is his own most amazing special effect.

What do you look for when you select your stuntmen?

I train them.

You train them yourself?

Yes. I have a young man who works for me now. When he first came on my team he was just a young kid, but he was not in my group yet. He just hangs the pads, sets up the safety things, and does those kinds of things until I think he's ready to join my group. Once I think he's good enough, then I'll bring him on my team. They know that if they keep at it, then one day they will have the chance to fight with me [on screen], which is so exciting to them. I mean, nobody else can fight with me in Asia. No matter how good the stuntmen are, they have to wait until I feel they are ready.

A superb martial artist and acrobat, Jackie has built his legend by putting his life on the line for his movies.

If you are the actor here, for example, and I'm talking to you, as soon as it is time to fight—"cut!"—and you are out. As soon as the fight begins you are out, I would replace you with a stuntman and change his hair to look like yours. My stuntmen fight with me because if you were to fight with me—no matter how good you are—we're unfamiliar with each other. So, when you kick or punch toward me, I'll be pulling away too soon, or maybe I'll be worrying about getting hit and, believe me, I've been hit too much already. I've been hurt so many times from people who were not my stuntmen; my nose has been broken three times because I trust people; my tooth is gone because the person I was fighting with did not have proper control of his technique, at least not as well as he needed it to be. I'm not saying that I still don't make mistakes. My own stuntmen have hurt me, too, but that's OK—I trust them—and that's an accident. If you hurt me or fight with me, then I'm scared [that an accident could happen]. But with my stuntmen, the chances of my getting injured are greatly reduced. We can go full out—[throws punches and kicks] bam! bam! bam! bam! bam!—we know each other's rhythm and timing!

If today, you find in America a very talented Caucasian stuntman, like you, or like anyone, to fight with me, it would be the worst-looking Jackie Chan fight scene of all time. Why? Because when you go to kick me, I'll be already flinching and turning away from you. If the scene calls for you to hit me across the back with a stick, I'm already covering up and trying to get away from you because I'm really scared that you are going to really hit me.

But my stuntmen can hit me right across my back with a club—boom!—and you can actually see it touch my shirt, and I'll stay there and take it because I know that he'll pull it just enough to prevent me from getting hurt. That's what we want in fight choreography. So that is why I always bring my stuntmen with me wherever I go. We have that timing together.

In *Rumble in the Bronx*, when they were throwing bottles at me in the alley sequence—boom! boom! boom!—I was able to trust them and tell them, "Come on, now, hit me right here on the arm with it," and they will. But if you were the one throwing the bottle at me, I'd rather be ten miles away because if I stood there, I might move a little bit because we're not used to each other—or you might not throw it where I'm expecting it—and I'll get hurt. So this is quite different from some of the other action stars who might use one set of stuntmen for one film, and then a second set of stuntmen for another film. How can you create realistic-looking fight scenes this way? You must fully trust the people you are working with, and you have to know each other, anticipate each other, and know each other's rhythm and timing. This is essential. You could put two good fighters together in a fight scene, but that doesn't necessarily mean it will be entertaining to watch in a movie. In the movies it's different fighting than

Using props such as bicycles for weapons has become a trademark of Jackie's films, like *Project A.*

what you would see, say, in a martial arts tournament or in a boxing match. There, it's bam! bam! bam! And that's a good fight to watch, too, they're really fighting and it's exciting. But in a movie, it's all rhythm, and that requires a different type of fighting. And even in the action stars' films, the actor doesn't want to get hurt, and says, "Don't hurt my nose, don't hit my face"—he's already scared! And that comes across in their films and really compromises their ability to fully express their character's personality or intention in their fighting scenes.

You have truly elevated stunt coordination and fight choreography into an art form. You have really infused an element of soul or honesty into your action sequences that keeps your character's scenes very pure.

The crew race to keep up with Jackie's car-leaping action during filming of *Mr. Nice Guy* in Melbourne, Australia.

Yes, well, I like action, but I hate violence. That's why in my movies you don't find a lot of violence. If you say, "Your movies are violent," I'll respond: "It's good violence; I didn't show the blood from the nose, there was no swearing"—like some other Hollywood stars' films, where every other scene is "F*** you! God damn!"—no, I never have any of this kind of dialogue. Also, I never have gunfights where there is someone shot—"Bang!"—and then blood comes pouring out of a guy's mouth, his nose, and so forth. So that is why when I design fighting scenes, it's more like an art, like dancing, rhythm. Like a tap dance, "ba-da-da-dum-dum, ba-da-da-dum-dum."

Given your upbringing in the Peking Opera and its very tough regimen, and the fact that you put your life on the line in many of your stunts in order to give your audience your best in every film you make, when you see a lot of the North American stuntmen who complain about doing stunts that are quite minor in comparison, does it upset you? Does it cause you to think "These guys don't know what hard work is"?

[emphatic] No. I think differently. I really learned my action, my punch—a lot of my punches in the movies—I really learned from American stuntmen in the beginning. Before, in the old days of the Hong Kong film industry, we were all fighting in a classical style—[performs a series of classical blocks and strikes] tung, tung, tung, tung—suddenly an American movie came to shoot in Hong Kong called *The Sand Pebbles* and it used a lot of Hong Kong stuntmen. They taught us how to do the reactions to a punch. It was a movie about a boat and a gunfight, and they used some Hong Kong actor. It was an American-made movie.

How long ago was this?

Oh, this would have been thirty-five or forty years ago. The American stuntmen gave a course to teach the Hong Kong stuntmen how to react properly to movie punches, and how to throw the punches. We learned how to do our reactions and our action from these American stuntmen.

And now it has come full circle as the Americans are looking to Hong Kong to learn new ways to do their stunts and fight scenes.

All those years ago we learned this much: reaction and punch. After that, we continued to create more things. However, in all of the years since then, the American moviemakers have been concentrating more on computer

"When I design fighting scenes, it's more like an art, like dancing, rhythm."—Jackie Chan

graphics and these kind of things, and staying away from what we were
working on developing because of unions and insurance considerations. Later
on, they went in more for big stunts, parachutes, crashing cars, motorcycle
jumps, and in those kinds of stunts America is still the best. We cannot do
those—parachuting, motorcycle jumping—because we don't have that kind
of room in Hong Kong. Even if you had a motorcycle, there's nowhere to
jump! Paragliding? Where? There's no space! So we worked on developing
the smaller things like kicking and punching. For fifty years, almost nonstop,
we've been working on improving our fighting action every day. Especially
me. So it's like going to school every day, how many things every day can I
create? Many things. Look at American movies. How many things are
created by computers? And they are the best at this. So now we learn from
America the special effects, and America learns from us the punching and
kicking, the small things.

**Do you think that a lot of American stunt coordinators copy a lot from
your movies?**

I believe right now that there are a lot of American stunt coordinators who
watch my movies. I can tell that when my movie is released in Asia they are
already looking at it. After that, they are releasing copies of my stunts and
action sequences in their own films before my movies are released in
America.

**What do you think of that—when you see stunts and action sequences that
you've created in your own mind and worked out with great effort and
meticulous detail on the screen, then ripped off by your American counterparts with absolutely no credit given to you?**

[smiles] I'm happy.

Really?

Yes, because I first learned from American stuntmen. After that I created my
own things. After I created my own things, somehow the technology in
films came up. I look at the videos of Buster Keaton and I think, "Wow!" I
find out that Buster Keaton and Harold Lloyd and I have the same kinds of
ideas for making movies. Then I found out that I had the same kind of talent.

Jackie uses an umbrella to hitch a ride on a speeding bus in his 1985 hit, *Police Story.*

But doesn't it upset you when you see, for example, Sylvester Stallone and Kurt Russell's film Tango and Cash *ripping off your bus stop/crash sequence?*

No!

But that's like your painting—something that you created. That doesn't upset you?

No, because I respect Stallone, I like him. He's my hero. Also, Spielberg is my hero. When I look at Spielberg's *Indiana Jones and the Temple of Doom,* I see that he totally copied my bicycle sequence from *Project A;* I used a bicycle, he used a motorcycle. But I'm so happy that even the biggest director has learned something from me! That makes me happy. But I have also learned from other movies. I just create my own things. I think that in the world of movies everybody copies everybody.

Leaping from the upper deck of a shopping mall onto a moving escalator was one of the more impressive—and dangerous—stunts that Jackie performed in *Police Story.*

I know that you damaged your ankle quite badly during the making of **Rumble in the Bronx.** *What happened?*

It was a pretty easy stunt. [laughing] For some reason I always seem to get hurt doing the easy stunts! That is what happened when we were filming *Armor of God* in Yugoslavia and I fell out of a tree and almost died. When I'm doing a big stunt I'm more careful, but the stunt in *Rumble* when I broke two bones was pretty small. I jumped from a bridge onto the deck of a hovercraft. When I landed, I was falling forward and would have banged my head on the cabin, so I turned as I landed. But the deck of the hovercraft is covered in a non-slip material, so while my body turned, my ankle didn't! [laughing] Go see the movie, it is much easier to see it than to talk about it! (JC/PNP)

You've obviously done so many fantastic stunts over the course of your career. But what stunt that you've done impresses you the most?

You're talking about big stunts? Nothing I've done impresses me that much. My kind of stunt, a lot of people can do it—it's just a question of whether or not the company will give you the right amount of money to do it, and whether you have the guts to do it or not. When I decide on a stunt for myself, I envision a first scene, second scene, chasing scene, and so on that pushes me to the limit. It pushes me to the point where the audience is saying, "Come on, do it, Jackie!" Then I just do the big stunt, and the audience goes "Yeah!" If I tell a lot of stunt guys to do the stunt, they will do it, they'll do the same thing because they'll be thinking, "Today is the day that *I'm* Jackie Chan. It will make me special."

"I think what I'm best at is choreography. It's more difficult than doing the stunts. Stunts are easy."
—Jackie Chan

I don't think the stunts are anything special. What I'm proud of is my choreography technique. My technique is more difficult than doing the stunt. You're talking about my jumping over a helicopter, hanging onto objects that are very high up—anybody can do that. I'm just being honest. But if you're talking about my technique, like doing a turning kick, coming down, throwing punches—boom! boom! boom!—and blending that with acting and comedy, that's more difficult than doing the stunt.

I think what I'm the best at is choreography. It's more difficult than doing the stunts. Stunts are easy. The difficult things are when I come back to the motor home on the set and have to plan out the techniques. How can I make the fighting exciting and still have comedy in it? And also, what can I do to get the audience all worked up to support me and want to see my character successfully do the stunt? The stunt is simple. By itself it's nothing, like drinking a coffee, or jumping over something—the audience would not get excited. Like, why are you drinking the coffee and then jumping over to the building? You have to have a setup like *Rumble in the Bronx*, where the people beat me and then chase me, and I climb up to the second floor, then to the third floor. They beat me again, beat me, beat me, beat me—I try to run away, but I've nowhere to go, and then I gesture to the bad guy to "Kiss my ass!" Then I run and do that big jump to the other building. The difficult part is not the stunt, it's the planning. The buildup to it. That's the difficult thing. That's my biggest talent.

"The difficult part is not the stunt, it's the planning. The buildup to it. That's the difficult thing. That's my biggest talent."—Jackie Chan

Anybody can do a stunt. My stuntboys all do great stunts, but why? Because they don't know how to choreograph. Why do they have to listen to me? Because I know these kinds of things, like, "No, that's too violent, put some comedy in there. OK, that's enough. Let me count—boom! boom! boom! boom!—No, too boring. Three punches here and one punch here. Break the glasses, move the table." Then they do the whole thing. Wrap. Go home. Then I do the editing in the car. Today the first shot, second shot. The whole thing comes together and I think, "Tomorrow, I should add two more things." Then, that's enough. Or I think about a stunt sequence. Say my character goes through a window. As soon as he goes through the window, a motorcycle comes rushing toward him. As soon as the motorcycle comes, I'll just touch the motorcycle and then turn over and fall down. And then the trucks will come at me, I'll get up, roll over the hood of the truck and fall off—and then a big truck comes. You go under the bridge and go to the coffee shop, and then you almost hit the person carrying the fruit juice, and he gets really frustrated and you say, "Sorry." And then the guy turns around and steps on a banana peel, then he falls down. Yes! You have to create the whole thing.

Do you carry around a pad of paper so that when the ideas for these things come to you, you can just write them down?

Yes.

Do you find yourself waking up at night with ideas and writing them down?

Yes. The paper is always beside my bed. I carry all the details with me everywhere I go. If I find something interesting, I write it down. But now it's getting easier. Now it's a lot of E-mails. I read a lot of books, even though I don't read English very well. If I find something helpful, I'll just copy it down. Then I'll put it up on my office wall. You can see that I have pictures of ideas for scenes all over my wall.

Over the years, Jackie's daredevil genius has matured as he continues to experiment with death-inviting, gravity-defying stuntwork which has almost finished his career and his life.

Appendix A

A Jackie Chan Filmography*

Year	Title	Type of Film
1971	*Little Tiger from Canton*	Martial Arts
1973	*Not Scared to Die*	Martial Arts
1973	*Heroine*	Martial Arts
1973	*All in the Family*	Martial Arts
1973	*In the Eagle's Shadow Fist*	Martial Arts
1976	*Countdown in Kung-Fu*	Martial Arts
1976	*New Fist of Fury*	Martial Arts
1976	*Shaolin Wooden Man*	Martial Arts
1977	*Killer Meteor*	Martial Arts
1977–78	*Snake and Crane Arts of Shaolin*	Martial Arts
1978	*To Kill with Intrigue*	Martial Arts
1978	*Half a Loaf of Kung-Fu*	Martial Arts

* does not include childhood roles

Jackie (right) and
boyhood chum Sammo
Hung (left) teamed up
together in the 1983 film
Project A.

1978	*The Magnificent Bodyguard*	Martial Arts
1978	*Snake in the Eagle's Shadow*	Comedy Kung Fu
1978	*Spiritual Kung-Fu*	Comedy Kung Fu
1978	*Dragon Fist*	Comedy Kung Fu
1978	*Drunken Master*	Comedy Kung Fu
1979	*The Fearless Hyena*	Comedy Kung Fu
1980	*Young Master*	Comedy Kung Fu
1980	*The Big Brawl*	Comedy Kung Fu
1981	*The Cannonball Run*	Action-Comedy
1982	*Dragon Lord*	Comedy Kung Fu
1983	*Winners and Sinners*	Action/Comedy
1983	*Project A*	Action/Comedy

Jackie (left) puts away another bad guy in *First Strike* (1996).

1984	*My Lucky Stars*	Action/Comedy
1984	*The Protector*	Action
1984	*Cannonball Run II*	Action/Comedy
1984	*Wheels on Meals*	Action/Comedy
1985	*Fantasy Mission Force*	Action
1985	*First Mission*	Action/Comedy
1985	*Police Story*	Action
1986	*Police Story II*	Action
1987	*Dragons Forever*	Action/Comedy
1988	*Armor of God*	Action/Comedy
1988	*Project A II*	Action/Comedy
1989	*Painted Faces* (cameo)	Semi-documentary

Jackie (right) kicks out at
British martial artist
Wayne Archer (left) in
1988's *Armor of God*.

1989	*Miracles* (a.k.a.: *Mr. Canton and Lady Rose*)	Action/Comedy
1990	*Armor of God II: Operation Condor*	Action/Comedy
1991	*Island of Fire* (cameo)	Action
1992	*City Hunter*	Comedy Kung Fu
1992	*Police Story III*	Action
1992	*Twin Dragons*	Comedy Kung Fu
1993	*Crime Story*	Action
1993	*Supercop II: Project S* (cameo)	Action
1994	*Drunken Master II*	Comedy Kung Fu
1995	*Rumble in the Bronx*	Action/Comedy
1995	*Thunderbolt*	Action
1996	*Police Story IV: First Strike*	Action/Comedy

1997	*Mr. Nice Guy*	Action/Comedy
1997	*Who Am I?*	Action/Comedy
1998	*Rush Hour*	Action/Comedy

The lobby poster for
Crime Story (1993)

Appendix B
Jackie Chan's Ten Greatest Stunts

When one literally puts his life on the line with every movie, it is hard to say one death-defying stunt is more worthy than the next. But among his electrifying body of work, there are ten instances where even the great Jackie teetered on the brink of ultimate disaster.

Because of New Line Cinema's aggressive marketing campaign with *Rumble in the Bronx,* Jackie Chan has now become an American household name. For those of us in America previously privy to his wild daredevilish antics and who could partake in secret conversations about the one we already knew was the best action-film star in the world, we are no longer special.

Sadly, we must now share our passion for Jackie's work with the rest of the country. But that's OK, because he deserves it. However, for those of us who truly appreciate and understand the martial arts—well, perhaps—that still makes us special.

Given Jackie's cinematic success, venturing to define his "top ten" stunts is almost ludicrous because, after all, how do you prioritize perfection? Therefore, the following choices are merely the opinions of a combination martial artist, movie fight choreographer, and Jackie Chan fan. While words alone can't do justice to the death-defying beauty of his onscreen best, they'll have to do. Seeing is believing.

1. Out on a Ledge

Stepping out onto the ledge of a clock tower, sixty feet above a group of nailbiting onlookers, Jackie prepares himself for what is about to be one of his most dangerous and best stunts to date. The cast and crew of *Project A*, Jackie's first "big" directorial effort, wonder if today is the day. They are waiting for him to do a stunt that straddles the line between courage and lunacy. *Project A* pits Marine Corps sergeant Ma Ru Lung and the Royal Hong Kong Navy against a ruthless band of South China Sea pirates in this madcap, nonstop turn-of-the-century romp.

In reality it is 1982, and Jackie Chan is the new king of Hong Kong cinema and Asia's top kung-fu star. Yet now he was becoming known as a comedy-action star who does his own stunts. The scene requires Jackie, who is cornered by pirates, to dangle Harold Lloyd–style from the clock's minute hand, let go, plummet through two cloth awnings, land on the ground, and walk away dumbfounded— all in one take, without wires, harnesses, mats, or the standard break-a-fall apparatus: cardboard boxes covered by a tatami (or mattress).

In *The Protector,* Jackie scales the scaffolding toward a crane—hundreds of feet above the ground!

Stunt-test preparation entailed tossing a sack of topsoil off the ledge. It worked, but of course a sack doesn't walk away from the fall, while Jackie had to. He could not be certain that the fall wouldn't kill him. How did he feel? He recalls thinking, "Scared, I just didn't want to go down." Production had halted for over a week as he daily stood on the ledge hardening himself. Then it happened. The clock face swung out, he let go of the minute hand and, per the scenario, tore through the first awning. However, instead of tearing through the second awning, he recklessly flopped off it, flipped upside-down, and flogged the ground headfirst.

Escaping serious injury, the words "Zai lai" (one more time) breached the precarious moment. A few days later Jackie tried the stunt again and it worked. He got up, walked toward the camera rubbing himself ("acting" like he was in pain), brandishing the typical face-folding grimace that has made him so famous.

2. A Pole Slide

As with any Jackie Chan film, it is his eye for creativity and finding the abnormally unobvious that keeps his audiences on their toes. In American films, whether it is a fight or a stunt, there always seems to be an insert shot of some apparatus or thing that lends to the predictability of a sequence's climax. If you have ever seen *Police Story*, nothing is predictable, whether it is the total annihilation of a hillside shantytown, or, his second best stunt, the fireman's pole gag. Admittedly his favorite film, Jackie plays the incessant inspector Chan Chia Chu as he takes on a powerful crime lord and his henchmen in a wild array of staggering set pieces and chases, climaxing with the film's most hair-raising moment.

Perched in a squatting position on a thin, slippery handrail, Jackie leaps ten feet out toward a pole. If he misses he would plummet seventy feet to his death—no safety nets and no wires, just air. Before the leap he yells out. It is not part of the script, it is the psyching-up yell of a madman ready to introduce himself to sane insanity. His maiden flight complete, he precariously hangs on to the pole, then slides down seventy feet through a meshwork of exploding Christmas-tree lights, crashes through a glass ceiling (used to break his fall), and lands spread-eagled on his back on the cold, cruel floor. In keeping with the spirit of *Project A*, within the same take, Jackie walks toward camera "acting" like he is hurt. Because of a misunderstanding, the propman had used house-current instead of a low-voltage car battery to light the bulbs. Jackie could have been electrocuted. He wasn't—but he does interject, "All the skin was peeled off from my hands." Certainly, not the first or last time Jackie would get burned.

Swinging from chandeliers is a piece of cake for the man who once hung from a rope ladder suspended from an airborne helicopter, dangling thousands of feet above the city of Kuala Lumpur.

3. Leap of Faith

In his most recognized work in America, *Rumble in the Bronx*, Jackie plays a cop who ends up protecting a storeowner who is harassed by a biker gang. Although martial arts pugilistic mayhem is sadly nominal, the film offers an array of far-out set pieces and some cumulatively over-the-top stuntwork that really pushed Jackie to the brink. His broken-ankled leap from a bridge onto a moving hovercraft and subsequent sneaker-painted sock are already legendary. But the most chilling—and his third best stunt—was his version of Stallone's crevice leap from *Cliffhanger*. The major differences here are that it is Jackie, it is between tall buildings, and there is no blue screen.

Trapped on a rooftop by pursuers, Jackie leaps to the balcony of an adjoining building, a drop of forty feet, to a three-foot target, twenty-six feet away. In fact, director Stanley Tong initially tried the stunt with a harness and concluded that it wouldn't look real. Instead, a twenty-four-foot-high platform was built on the second floor for Jackie to rehearse on, enabling him to calibrate the exact path he would have to run before leaping. The path was then marked with tape on top of

Jackie shows his skill on a snowboard in *First Strike* (1996).

the roof of the building and he executed the blind leap with nothing but an air bag to cushion his fall if he missed and fell eight floors to the ground. Astoundingly, it took one take.

4. Another Leap

As with any of his stunts, each setup is purposely designed to provide heart-stopping proof of Jackie's commitment to his audience. This is no more evident than in his homage to Indiana Jones, *Armor of God*, which features his fourth best stunt. Lacking the extravagant inventiveness of its higher-budgeted sequel, the film is mostly known for his close bout with death and the resulting hole in his head from a simple stunt gone awry.

Yet Jackie's everlasting commitment to creativity and originality constantly requires him to learn and master new skills that seemingly require him to go one step beyond the norm. By kidnapping his ex-girlfriend, machine gun-toting monks force Jackie to steal the remaining pieces of the "armor of the god" so the monks can make the world safe for the forces of darkness. Jackie decides to storm their

The stunning car chase from *Police Story* proceeds down a steep hill and through an unsuspecting shantytown.

dungeonic castle and rescue everybody, in an ending that pits him in a hacking-and-whacking food fight with a bunch of martial-artist monks. It is a painful-to-watch, ultra-cool confrontation with a quartet of busty, stiletto-heeled amazon women dressed in leather.

For this final stunt in *Armor of God*, Jackie had to learn skydiving. But it wasn't enough for him merely to learn and do a few jumps; he had to use his own madcap method. Leaping off a mountaintop and—while in mid-air—landing onto a passing-by passenger balloon, he then lowers himself into the passenger's basket by climbing down the side of the balloon. Basically, the parachute was there in case he missed the balloon. But demented Jackie strikes again. You would think that after recovering from his bad fall he would have held back a little for this stunt. But as psycho as his sight gags are, *Armor* changed his views about stunts. "Before, I just worried about the big stunts in every film, but then, after that," he said, "I realized that every stunt is a serious one."

5. Plan of Attack

In *Police Story III: Supercop* Jackie teams up with a Mainland police inspector played by Michelle Khan for a joint Hong Kong–PRC mission to topple a notorious druglord. Jackie's fifth best stunt, the breathtaking car/motorcycle/helicopter/train finale, is nothing short of miraculous. Although his fight sequences are always created on the set without preproduction and storyboards, dangerous stunts usually are planned out well in advance. However, not to be outdone by the marvelous stuntwork Michelle performed when she rode her motorbike off a steep hill and landed on a speeding train full of baddies, Jackie whimsically decided to once again go for broke. He chose to leap off a building, grab a rope ladder dangling from an airborne helicopter, dangle a thousand feet over the city of Kuala Lumpur, and then, to top it off, have the pilot smash his body against a building's lofty spire, crash him through a high-rise's billboard, and drop him onto the same moving train. Recently Jackie recalled on *The Rosie O'Donnell Show*, "It was amazing, we had this guy who had flown during the Vietnam War. I was up there for fifteen days hanging onto that rope. But for safety I did wear a harness—a thousand feet is a long way down."

Jackie in *Police Story* (1985)

6. A Traffic Stop

Unlike the first five stunts, whose cinematic thrill relies on a combination of Jackie's individual ability and multiple takes from multiple camera angles repeated in quick succession, his sixth best stunt is presented in an almost subliminal fashion and ambushes the viewer. In *Police Story II*, Jackie has been demoted to traffic cop for his hijinks in the first *Police Story* and must somehow find a way to bust a crew of serial bombers while maintaining his ever-fragile relationship with Maggie Cheung. It's fast, furious, and delirious.

As Jackie comically scampers across a busy Hong Kong main road flooded with cars, he leaps over the highway divider and is supposed to be nailed by an oncoming van. He must rely on the stunt driver to stop at a preset point. What is so neat about this stunt is that if you watch Jackie carefully he is not only *not* looking in the direction of the oncoming vehicle but, in an attempt to minimize the impact, he doesn't even try to lean away from the van prior to the collision. He literally jumps in front of the van, hoping that the driver stops it in time. Jackie laughingly recalls, "I remember the stuntdriver didn't stop where he was supposed to, so he hit me full force with the car. He felt so bad, but I told him that he did a good job." Landing in front of the van upon contact, Jackie careens off to the side, literally flying out of frame. It's wild to witness.

7. Undisputed Classic

In a masterful follow-up to *Project A*, *Project A II* displays Jackie's seventh best stunt, although the handcuff scene in *Project A* remains an undisputed classic. In *Project A II*, we find Jackie's hot-shot naval hero Ma Ru Lung caught up in a complex crisscrossing web of corruption and espionage involving everyone from corrupt cops and gangsters to antigovernment rebels and government hit men plus a band of angry pirates left over from the first film.

For the birthday of Tian Ho Niang Niang (a famous female goddess), the townfolk are building a huge makeshift temple. Unfortunately the two main, fifty-foot-tall billboard-like walls are loosely connected. After beating up Ching Dynasty subversives in and around the scaffolding from atop one of the walls, Jackie sees the traitorous inspector getting away. He straddles one of the wobbly walls, forcing it to tilt to one side. As the wall leans one way and then falls down like a chopped tree, Jackie runs down the side of the wall opposite to the direction of the fall. When the wall reaches the ground, he simply runs off it as if he had just run down a ramp. Meanwhile, the other wall is toppling down toward him. In a

The action in a Jackie
Chan film is always on
the highest possible order.

direct salute to Buster Keaton's *Steamboat Willie*, the side of the building crashes
onto Jackie with only one small paper-covered window preventing him from being
squashed like a bug. He humorously thanks the female goddess for protecting him.

8. Waterworld of Horror

It is said that one way to conquer fear is to face it. The one thing that Jackie dis-
likes most is having to do stuff in water. It is painfully obvious in *Police Story IV: First
Strike* that Jackie is an extremely weak swimmer. Yet he challenges his "fear" to the
max, going beyond what any of us would do in water even if we were great swim-
mers. Jackie's astonishing stunts obviously lack Hollywood's safety elements and are
filmed in a way that guarantees their absolute authenticity. In part four of the
adventures of Detective Chan, for the first time without Maggie Cheung, we see
Jackie trying to prevent nuclear armaments from getting into the wrong hands.
Apart from some wacky snowboarding stunts à la James Bond, fighting with a ten-
foot folding ladder, and hanging out on very tall building ledges, Jackie's eighth best

Underwater fight in a shark tank? Jackie shows how it's done during *First Strike.*

stunt is essentially a combination of all the film's wild and woolly, sometimes chilly, rock 'em—sock 'em, shark-infested water gags and pranks.

Chan and company choreographed some over-the-top, totally humorous fight sequences that were shot entirely underwater. He battles scuba-diver hitmen, feeding off their oxygen tanks when the fight allowed him to do so, while a school of man-eating sharks swam overhead. Other water stunts include a forty-foot drop into a chilling, ice-encrusted lake. One may think that Jackie is overacting during the days of shooting in sub-zero temperatures, but he comically reveals that he doesn't need to act for he is wearing sub-par clothing. His cute two-eyed, baby-seal-looking woolen hat is just the sort of thing that reminds us that he still doesn't take himself seriously—he is being himself. And with his "docudrama" style of outtakes so vividly displayed at the film's end, this brings his contribution to the films up to another level of discipline and dedication, reflects his willingness to fight for success, and amplifies his pledge to audience satisfaction.

9. "He Just Did It"

The last two stunts pay homage to Jackie's gutsy psyche during a period when time, money, and technology were all lacking in his arsenal of filmmaking weapons. They were times when all you really did was go for it and worry about the consequences later, regardless of what they might be. The year was 1981 and I'm [Reid] busy working on a kung-fu film in Taiwan getting my butt kicked in by the hero. During one of the breaks, the stuntmen were talking about a film being shot in central Taiwan where many of the stuntmen were literally breaking their necks. I already knew that working in these films had minimal safety requirements, but I thought I must have misinterpreted the stuntmen's Mandarin Chinese. They talked about a three-story-high, pyramidal wooden frame where about fifty guys were supposed to be climbing to the top. One of the actors, upon almost reaching the top, purposely let go and rolled backward over a sea of clamoring stuntmen. He smashed into the ground and was dragged off. The film was *Dragon Lord* and the free-falling stuntman was Jackie Chan. It was Jackie's final tribute to his kung fu mold and featured his ninth best stunt.

Jackie made his mark internationally through his stuntwork in *Dragon Lord*. The film, where workers literally were breaking their necks, featured Jackie climbing to the top of a pyramid-like structure and then purposely letting go. He rolled over backward, smashed into the ground, and was dragged off.

There was no planning, storyboarding, or preparation—he just did it. Basically the main villain, played by Wang Ing Sik (best known as the Japanese villain in Bruce Lee's *Return of the Dragon*), is a one-eyed traitor selling Chinese antiques to the evil foreigners. Spotlighting a soccer-style, hackey-sack melee, a rugby-like kamikaze routine, and a first-rate barn battle that knocks you (and him) out, the film won Jackie critical acclaim as one of the most-celebrated (and perhaps craziest) stuntworkers in the industry. The outtakes at the end of the film, a result of his *The Cannonball Run* films and now an essential part of the Chan film experience, also show Jackie falling headfirst into the ground from high balconies, without using safety equipment, wires, harnesses, or mats. The film set the pace for things to come, and come they did.

10. Hurled from a Harness

"I like action, but I hate violence. That's why in my movies you don't find a lot of violence."—Jackie Chan

Chan's final best stunt is his first best stunt. It's 1972, and a young Jackie Chan is being fitted into a harness. One end of a single piece of wire is attached to his harness and the other end is inserted through a series of pulleys and tied onto a long, thick piece of rope. When signaled, three guys grab the rope, pull, and run like

hell, forcing Jackie skyward. Without body padding, he is blindly hurled backward about twenty feet and smashingly dumped onto solid concrete, and a star stuntman was born. Jackie was doubling for the character Mr. Suzuki in the final scene of *The Chinese Connection* when a flying Bruce Lee kicked Jackie's body through a window and into the limelight. If only Bruce were alive today to see what we have seen since!

Over the years, Jackie's daredevil genius matured as he continued to experiment with death-inviting, gravity-defying stuntwork that has—at many times—almost finished his career and life. His astonishing stunts obviously lack Hollywood's safety features and are filmed in such a way that the camera guarantees their absolute authenticity. Jackie has an uncanny ability to cleverly reveal humorous movements and facial expressions, while concealing the dangers exhibited in his death-defying work. The stunts are indeed thrilling because no one in his right mind would attempt them.

Jackie Chan's next greatest challenge will be how he handles the unavoidable and irreversible effects of age. But in answer to that he humbly states, "My body is always in pain and I know I can't do this when I am sixty-two. But I will keep going as long as I can, and as long as I enjoy it. To me, doing this is like a hobby; it is something I do for fun." And that's what Jackie is all about. The action in his films produces an authentic, startling rush of excitement where the unabated pleasure and exhilaration of moviegoing is reborn close to its purest form—fun. (JC/10GS)

—Dr. Craig D. Reid

Notes on Text

1. Raymond Chow is the founder of Hong Kong's Golden Harvest Studios, the film company that has produced almost all of Jackie Chan's movies.

2. Writing of Bak Mei in her book *The Complete Guide to Kung-Fu Fighting Styles*, Jane Hallander says, "White eyebrow is usually referred to as a short, middle-hand system. The arms are flexible and soft until contact is made, then they are sharp and sudden with a penetrating power. The strength or power in white eyebrow is referred to as 'sudden' or 'scared' power and, unlike many other martial arts, the white eyebrow practitioner's power is released only upon impact. Prior to actual impact, his hand movements are soft. The white eyebrow stylists derive much of their power and flexibility from waist action, more so than do some other short hand styles, such as wing chun." (*The Complete Guide to Kung-Fu Fighting Styles*, Jane Hallander, Unique Publications, 1985, p. 101)

3. Sammo Hung met Jackie when they were both youngsters indentured at the Peking Opera school in Hong Kong. Sammo, under the stage name Yuen Chu, was the lead member of opera children who included "brothers" Jackie and Yuen Biao. A gifted stunt coordinator and martial artist in his own right, Sammo has most recently directed Jackie in the movie, *Mr. Nice Guy*.

4. The term "brothers," as Jackie uses it, refers to his close childhood friends (many of whom have gone on to make names for themselves in Hong Kong action films) from his ten years in the Peking Opera.

5. In Jackie's autobiographical videotape, *The Jackie Chan Story*, released from Media Asia, he is shown working out with Ken Lo on focus gloves, Thai pads, and a foam shield in the manner that he describes here.

6. Jackie is being too modest, as the price he has paid physically has been far more than "broken fingers" and a "broken ankle." To date, Jackie has had his right eye scratched and left eye cut, his hair singed and burned, his skull fractured and eyebrows burned off; suffered partial hearing loss in his right ear; had his nose broken three times, his jaw dislocated, his face cut and scarred, his upper lip cut, a cap knocked out of a tooth, his neck sprained, his collarbone fractured, his shoulder pulled, his back sprained, both elbows broken, his hands slashed and burned, five fingers broken, ribs cracked, back twisted, a hip dislocated, a leg punctured, a foot broken, an ankle broken and several toes broken—and he has plenty of movies left to go!

7. Lau Chia Liang has directed some very well-received martial arts films, including *36th Chamber of Shaolin* and *Legendary Weapons of Kung Fu*.

8. Wong Fei Hung was a legendary Chinese folk hero, comparable to the Lone Ranger and Sherlock Holmes. He was a master martial artist who was born in Canton Province in 1847 and died in 1924 at the age of 77. In the winter of 1949, the first Chinese language film about the exploits of Wong Fei Hung, *The True Story of Wong Fei Hung*, was shot by the Yong Yao Film Company. This film launched a series of some ninety-nine epic films. More recently there have been new films released featuring the Wong Fei Hung character, including two by Jackie Chan—*Drunken Master* and *Drunken Master II*, the latter being the greatest hit in Southeast Asia in 1994.

9. Korea is traditionally one of the greatest markets for Hong Kong action films. Buyers there would buy unseen any action film, especially one with Jet Li, Chow Yun-Fat, or Cynthia Khan. However, in recent years, audiences are responding only to high-quality action films.